01253 504635

Seated Acupressure Bodywork

a practical handbook for therapists

Andrew Parfitt

D0319753

Lotus Publishing
Chichester, England

North Atlantic Books
Berkeley, California

BLACKPOOL AND THE FYLDE COLLEGE

3 8049 00132 278 6

Copyright© 2006 by Andrew Parfitt. All rights reserved. No portion of this book, except for brief review, may be reproduced, stored in a retrieval system, or transmitted in any form or by any means electronic, mechanical, photocopying, recording, or otherwise without the written permission of the publisher. For information, contact Lotus Publishing or North Atlantic Books.

First published in 2006 by
Lotus Publishing
9 Roman Way, Chichester, PO19 3QN and
North Atlantic Books
P O Box 12327
Berkeley, California 94712

All Drawings Amanda Williams
Text Design Wendy Craig
Cover Design Chris Fulcher
Printed and Bound in the UK by The Bath Press

Disclaimer

This book is intended to accompany a professional training course and cannot replace tuition by a qualified teacher. The author accepts no liability for injuries caused by misinterpretation of techniques described in the following pages.

Acknowledgements

I cannot make a claim to originality or creation of any of the techniques or information contained in this book but have simply collated and written down some of what I have learnt over the last 20 years since I began studying Martial Arts and Oriental medicine. My thanks go to all my teachers over the years without whose help and guidance I would not have been able to compile this book.

Seated Acupressure Bodywork is sponsored by the Society for the Study of Native Arts and Sciences, a non-profit educational corporation whose goals are to develop an educational and cross cultural perspective linking various scientific, social, and artistic fields; to nurture a holistic view of arts, sciences, humanities, and healing; and to publish and distribute literature on the relationship of mind, body, and nature.

British Library Cataloguing in Publication Data
A CIP record for this book is available from the British Library
ISBN 1 905367 02 3 (Lotus Publishing)
ISBN 1 55643 624 6 (North Atlantic Books)

Library of Congress Cataloguing-in-Publication Data
    Parfitt, Andrew.
 Seated acupressure bodywork : a practical handbook for therapists / Andrew Parfitt.
    p. ; cm.
 Includes bibliographical references and index.
  ISBN 1-55643-624-6 (pbk. : alk. paper) -- ISBN 1-905367-02-3 (pbk. : alk. paper)
 1. Massage therapy--Handbooks, manuals, etc. 2. Job stress--Prevention--Handbooks, manuals, etc. 3. Job stress--Treatment--Handbooks, manuals, etc.
 [DNLM: 1. Massage--methods--Handbooks. 2. Stress, Psychological--prevention & control--Handbooks. 3. Stress, Psychological--therapy--Handbooks. 4. Workplace--psychology--Handbooks. WB 39 P229h 2006] I. Title.
  RM721.P25 2006
  615.8'22--dc22
                        2005034733

Contents

Introduction   5

1   What is Seated Acupressure Bodywork?   7

2   An Overview of Oriental Medicine   9

3   Stress in the Workplace   29

4   Screening Clients and Contraindications to
     Seated Acupressure Bodywork   35

5   Recommendations for Seated Acupressure Bodyworkers   41

6   The 20-Minute Seated Acupressure Bodywork Sequence   47

7   Working the Legs   93

8   Maximizing the Benefits of Seated Acupressure Bodywork   97

9   East Meets West: Adapting Swedish Massage for Use in an
     On-site Situation   107

10   Managing and Marketing Your Practice   113

     Appendix 1   The 10-Minute Routine   117

     Appendix 2   Sample Screening and Contraindication Form   119

     Appendix 3   Summary of the 20-Minute Seated Acupressure
                       Bodywork Sequence   121

     Appendix 4   A Guide to Cun Measurements   135

     Bibliography   137

     Useful Addresses   139

     Index   141

Introduction

Since its development in the 1980's, seated acupressure bodywork has spread rapidly across the world. More and more people are becoming familiar with massage in a chair and it is not uncommon these days to see therapists with their chairs in shopping centres, and department stores, as well as at airports, exhibitions, and at health and trade fairs. Treatment can also be offered in the workplace, as well as from private clinics. On-site (seated acupressure bodywork) massage is fun to do and to learn, and is of immense value in these driven and stressful times.

It is however important that members of the public who are thinking of receiving any form of complementary therapy can trust the practitioner they consult. There are several schools teaching on-site massage or seated acupressure bodywork courses, which are accredited by a range of complementary therapy associations. I would recommend that anyone considering having treatment or employing the services of a seated acupressure therapist for their company thoroughly checks the training and insurance cover of the therapist. Similarly if you are considering learning this fascinating therapy, you should look into the background of the school and the teachers with whom you are going to study.

Having a good sound understanding of human anatomy and physiology is just as essential in a bodywork practitioner as the ability to apply the physical techniques to the body. When using acupressure massage it is also necessary to have an understanding of the general principles of Oriental medicine. It is one thing to know where certain points are located and how to stimulate them, but without understanding the theory behind them, the treatments you are giving will almost always affect your client on a superficial level only. Knowledge of why you are doing certain things will give you the ability to affect the client at a much deeper and more lasting level.

It is not possible to learn a hands-on therapy like seated acupressure bodywork from a book as certain subtle nuances of the techniques used cannot be adequately described in pictures and writing, but need to be explained, demonstrated and experienced. This book started life as a handout to accompany a seated acupressure bodywork course and subsequently took on a life of its own, growing into what I hope will be a useful guide to this wonderful art. It should not be used to replace tuition by a qualified and experienced teacher, but should be used as a reference book and as a reminder of the techniques you have learned on a structured course.

Along with a detailed description, using both words and illustrations of the 20-minute seated acupressure bodywork sequence, I have included a few extra techniques that I have found to be both effective and pleasant to receive. I would encourage you to experiment with, and explore different techniques, and incorporating techniques from other systems. Bodywork is a living thing, each and every person will be different and no one person will be absolutely the same when you see him or her for a second time. Learn to adapt and be flexible but never forget the basic technique sequence upon which your treatments are based.

CHAPTER 1

What is Seated Acupressure Bodywork?

Quite simply, on-site massage or seated acupressure bodywork is a 20-minute massage given through the clothes of a client who is seated in a specially designed chair. The session is often given at the client's workplace; hence the term 'on-site'.

Seated acupressure bodywork was developed in Silicon Valley in California in 1984 when David Palmer began giving 15-minute head, neck and shoulder massages to employees of Apple Computers. So successful was this venture that he designed an ergonomic portable massage chair to enable him to give a better and far more effective massage to his clients who were seated in total comfort.

Since then, seated acupressure bodywork has travelled across the world and has become increasingly popular. There are many reasons for this but first and foremost, it works! Research has shown that just twenty minutes of this enjoyable and stress relieving therapy can promote health and reduce sickness levels.

One of the advantages of seated acupressure bodywork is that it is performed through the receiver's clothes. This removes the concern some people have about undressing in front of a stranger and the possibility of unwelcome touch. It also reduces the time it takes for a massage as the therapist can come to you at your office. No oils or lotions are used.

Although seated acupressure bodywork was designed for use in the office, it is becoming more and more available in a wide range of outlets from special back rub shops to airports, fitness centres, beauty salons, hotels, conference centres and even on the beach. The potential is limitless.

The seated acupressure bodywork sequence is based on the Traditional Chinese massage called anma. Anma literally means; 'push – pull' or 'press – rub' in Chinese. Anma is a healing system that can be traced back over 2500 years to the time of Huang-ti, the legendary Yellow Emperor. It is a system of Oriental massage that, in a similar way to acupuncture, focuses on the balance and flow of Qi around the body through a complex system of channels or meridians. Anma was introduced to Japan from China about 1500 years ago.

Up until the Edo period about 300–400 years ago, all Japanese doctors were required to study anma as a way of familiarising themselves with the anatomy and musculature of the human body. Blind practitioners often practiced anma, as it was one of the few professions they could follow and their sense of touch was often heightened as a result of their lack of sight. Over the years this practice declined and anma eventually became licensed only for pleasure and relaxation. During the 20th century the Japanese government started to tax the anma practitioners and so a group of practitioners developed a new therapy that they called shiatsu. Shiatsu integrated the pressing and rubbing techniques of anma with the joint manipulations of Western physiotherapy and the meridian and point system used in acupuncture to create a comprehensive healing system.

There are several schools teaching seated acupressure bodywork but the sequence, form, or 'Kata' remains very similar, each one having their own unique nuances. The routine or Kata outlined in this book combines aspects of shiatsu and anma in a practical form that enables the practitioner to move around the body in a particularly flowing way.

In the West, the term Kata is usually associated with martial arts but in Japan the word has far more meaning. Katas are studied in all of the traditional Japanese arts, rituals and ceremonial practices from making tea to flower arranging and from dancing to the often complex empty hand and weapons forms used in martial arts practice.

On a very practical level, the study of a Kata enables us to learn our massage without having to think too deeply about the intricacies of what we are doing. As we practice the Kata more and more, it becomes a discipline that becomes automatic, enabling us to move on to a higher level of understanding about massage, touch and our ability to help those we are working with. The more you practice a particular form or Kata, the more natural, flowing and beneficial it will become. Think of the Kata as a dance. Then, just as your client will feel the benefit of a smooth and flowing treatment, so too will your own Qi feel the results.

The advantages of learning a Kata also cross into the area of business. If you intend to work alone it is not an issue if you wish to vary your routine, ad-lib or add in extra techniques. In fact we are in no way suggesting that you stick entirely to the routine and do not try to learn new or better ways of working. However if you are working for a large company, the advantages of being able to perform a routine that is identical to that being used by your colleagues means that clients will get a consistent and high quality treatment from whoever they see.

The routine has been designed to take about 20 minutes and covers the back, neck, shoulders, head, arms and hands of the client. The routine involves the use of about sixty acupressure points as well as stretches and joint mobilizations and is a revitalizing, tonifying and uplifting experience. The sequence promotes a sense of wellbeing because muscles relax, blood circulation is increased and nerve responses are stimulated: and through the meridian system and acupressure points, the organs of the body are tonified. Whilst not designed as a corrective treatment, regular users often report a lessening of any symptoms they may have been experiencing.

Due to this stimulating effect, regular seated acupressure bodywork will help to keep the body in peak condition. Most of us will have our cars regularly serviced to keep them in tip-top condition, so why not do the same for our bodies?

CHAPTER 2
An Overview of Oriental Medicine

Qi, the Meridians and Acupressure Points

The theory behind seated acupressure bodywork is firmly rooted in Oriental medicine. The ancient Chinese developed a very philosophical approach to their health that is just as appropriate today as it was 2500 years ago. The Chinese were in fact great believers in preventative medicine, and many of the richer classes would retain personal physicians to keep them healthy with a mix of massage, herbs, acupuncture, moxibustion, cupping, exercise, dietary advice, and meditation. The penalties for failure in ancient China could be severe, and the physician would not be paid when or if their employer became ill, and in some extreme cases their lives may have been in danger.

The theory of Chinese medicine revolves around the flow of Qi or energy through the body. In health, this Qi flows in a continuous 24-hour cycle around the body through a system of channels or meridians. All along these meridians are energy points (acupressure or acupuncture points), where the Qi can easily be accessed or influenced.

Good health is dependent on the harmonious flow of Qi around the body to carry nourishment and life to where it is needed, just as a river network will carry nourishment to the land. If the current in a river becomes blocked, upstream the pressure will build up, putting the banks under strain, and downstream there will be a lack of water and life will start to suffer. Similarly, when the flow of Qi becomes disrupted in the channels, the result can be stagnation or blockage of energy causing localized pain and a deficiency or atrophy in the channel downstream. If the disruption occurs in, or reaches the organs of the body, the functions of that organ will be compromised and symptoms of dis-ease can result which will vary according to the organ that is affected.

Qi is essentially our life force: it is what gives us life and enables us to eat, breathe, move, and think. Oriental philosophy believes that Qi permeates every thing in the universe, whether living or non-living.

Traditionally in the East, the Body, Mind and Spirit are interlinked and inseparable, and affect one another on all levels. Thus emotional problems can manifest on a very physical level and the physical will affect the emotions. We all know how aches and pains can leave you feeling grumpy or how grief can leave you with a very real aching in the chest area.

There are many factors which can affect the Qi: emotions, external factors such as the weather, e.g. extreme damp or heat, pressures of work, lifestyle excesses, diet, excess exercise or sexual activity, illness or injury, surgery, medical misdiagnosis, or overuse of drugs, both prescribed and recreational. Any of these can cause an imbalance in the body, but in practice there is usually a combination of factors underlying any one problem.

Yin and Yang

In ancient China, Daoist scholars believed that Qi, the vital energy that flows through and motivates every thing in the universe, is divided into two complementary and contradictory forces. These opposing forces were named Yin and Yang. Yin represents the substantial, female, negative, darker, softer, moister, inactive, and restful aspect of things. Yang represents the insubstantial, male, positive, brighter, harder, drier, more dominant, and active aspects. Thus, night-time is considered more Yin, whereas daytime is more Yang. Furthermore, Yin and Yang are in a constant state of flux, always trying to maintain equilibrium and harmony. For example, in this world night inevitably becomes day and always returns to night again. It must also be remembered that Yin and Yang can only be seen in relation to one another, for example hot can only be considered Yang when compared to something more Yin, e.g. cold.

Figure 2.1: The T'ai-Ji symbol.

According to Chinese Daoist philosophy, the rhythm of life that courses through the universe is the action of the complementary principles of Yin and Yang. The T'ai-Ji symbol (*see* figure 2.1) illustrates this principle. The dark outer circle is said to represent the unity of the universe. The symmetrical distribution of the dark Yin and the light Yang suggests a cyclical change, with the Yang energy descending and the Yin energy rising. When Yin reaches its climax, it recedes allowing Yang to ascend: after Yang reaches its climax, it recedes in favour of Yin. This is a continuous or eternal cycle. The dots inside the white and black halves indicate that within each is the seed of the other. Yin cannot exist without Yang and each contains the potential for the growth of the other.

The ideal state of things in the physical universe, as well as in the world of humans is a state of harmony, represented by the balance of Yin and Yang in body and mind.

> '*Yin-Yang is the Way of Heaven and Earth, the fundamental principle of the myriad things, the father and mother of change and transformation, the root of inception and destruction.*'
> Su-wen

Some of the characteristics of Yin and Yang are summarized in the following table.

Yang	Yin
Yang is the strong, masculine, creative and giving force that is associated with heaven. The energy of heaven above us is continuously in motion and brings about change. Yang energy is often associated with the following:	Yin is the female, intuitive, quiet and receptive force and is associated with earth. The earth is the source of life, it provides us with the nourishment and support we need to survive and grow. Yin is associated with the following:
- Light and Daytime	- Night and Darkness
- Fire and Heat	- Rain, Water, Cold
- Summer, Spring	- Winter, Autumn
- Even Numbers	- Odd Numbers
- The Sun and Sunshine	- The Moon and Moonlight
- South	- North
- Upwards	- Down
- Intellect	- Intuition
- Active, Dynamic	- Passive, Static
- Expansion, Increasing	- Contraction, Decreasing
- Exterior	- Interior
- Innovative, Reformative	- Traditional, Conservative
- Mountain	- Valley
- Desert	- River
- Straight Lines	- Curves
- Hard	- Soft
- Dissolving	- Solidifying
- Psychological World, Ethereal	- Physical World, Earthly
- Bladder, Small and Large Intestines, Skin	- Kidneys, Heart, Liver, Lungs, Spleen

The Theory of the Five Elements

Daoist sages in ancient China sought to explain the structure of change in the natural world. Living simple lives closely connected with their natural environment, they observed the changes in nature, the seasons progressing in an orderly way, and in the growth and development of all living things.

They noticed also how these changes occurred in Humans in an orderly way as they progressed from birth through infancy, puberty, adolescence, and adulthood, and into old age. They noticed also how it is not only the physical aspects of life that follow these cycles, but also how our personal psychology follows consistent patterns. Consequently, they came up with the idea that change is not a random thing but occurs in an organised pattern.

From their observations they formulated the idea of the five transformations or Five Elements, as they have become known. This is a philosophical way of looking at life: a way of trying to understand life and the universe. In ancient China the Five Elements were used for everything from medicine and healing, agriculture, economics and politics, war, divination and predicting the weather.

When you look at the principles of Yin and Yang, it is clear that the ancient Daoists looked at the natural world as existing in a constant state of change. Yin-Yang theory looks at the dual polarity of Qi or the relationship between opposite forces which are interdependent and complementary to each other, whilst able to consume and transform into each other.

The Five Elements, or more correctly, The Five Phase theory, is a development of this and shows the progression from pure energy to matter or thoughts, and ideas into things of substance.

First there was One
The One became Two
The Two became Five
And the Five became the 10,000 things

The One was the universal energy or Qi; the Two are Yin and Yang; the Five are the Elements; and the 10,000 things are everything in the universe (10,000 being a number the Chinese used to imply an infinite number of things).

According to this theory, all phenomena are a combination or products of the interaction and movement of these five Elements: Water, Wood, Fire, Earth and Metal. These five Elements are not necessarily the physical constituents of matter but are an energetic expression of the changes that occur throughout the universe.

The five phases were first described from a medical aspect in the *Huang Di Nei Jing* or *Yellow Emperor's Treatise on Internal Medicine*, which was written around 535 BC. According to this book, which is still used as a textbook in colleges of Oriental medicine, each of the Elements has a set of correspondences that occur throughout nature and the human body.

Water

Water is often considered the first, most enduring and flexible stage of the cycle. Water symbolises continuity of change whilst moving towards a specific goal. On earth, Water constantly flows towards the oceans. Yet Water also has the ability to mould itself into any contour or shape and find a place of balance. It has the power of utter stillness. In the Five Element Theory, the Water phase is associated with decline, with winter, with rest, and with latent hidden power. It is associated with our drive and will to live and procreate. In the Water stage, seeds lie dormant, waiting, building their resources, ready to burst forth in the spring. The organs of the Water element are the Kidneys and Bladder. It is associated with our basic instinct of fight or flight and the emotion of fear. People with issues around their Water element may have a blue / black colour on their faces, particularly under the eyes. Other associations are the ears, salty taste, a putrid smell, and a groaning voice. Water energy descends. The climatic association of Water is cold.

Wood

The Wood stage is the realisation of our dreams. Seeds that lay dormant during the winter suddenly sprout, and plants start to grow. An acorn, despite its size, contains the blueprint for an oak tree, and the same can be said about any seed. On a psychological level, an idea planted in our minds is nourished by a healthy Wood element, which gives us the ability for planning and decision-making, enabling us to turn our dreams into reality. Wood bears fruits that provide nourishment for us. It feeds fires with its branches, and its seeds and leaves fertilize the soil, thus allowing regeneration and the process to start again. The Wood element is about flexibility, and when balanced, this is reflected in our ligaments, tendons and joints, and also in our mental capacity to deal with change. Thus, when this element is out of balance, people are likely to be physically and emotionally rigid. Other associations are the colour green, spring, rancid smell and sour taste, anger and irritability, a shouting voice, and the eyes. Wood is about the free flow of energy. The climatic association of Wood is wind.

Fire

The Fire stage is the summer. It is about warmth, joy and compassion. In nature it is a time of ripening of crops or maturity. In humans our Fire element is responsible for how we see ourselves and how we relate to others and deal with relationships. Associations with Fire include the Heart and Small Intestines, joy and a laughing sound, a bitter taste, a scorched smell and the colour red. The external organ of the Fire element is the tongue, and people with an imbalance may have a tendency to open their hearts too freely even with strangers or equally to have a speech impediment like a stammer or lisp. Fire energy rises and warms. The climatic association of Fire is heat.

Earth

The Earth element is about nourishment and our connection to the ground. In terms of seasons, it is the late summer period and is connected with harvest and fertility. The Earth period is when the ideas we had start to take shape and form, come into being or into the realm of the physical world. The organs associated with the Earth element are the Spleen and Stomach, and so Earth is about the intake of food, nourishment and digestion. This also implies digestion of information as well, because the Earth gives us the power of intellectual thought and concentration. (This is called the Yi, in Oriental medicine). The emotional aspect of Earth is sympathy or pensiveness, and earthy people will often be very good listeners but may also have a tendency to worry excessively. Other associations are the colour yellow, which can often be seen on the face or around the mouth. The voice will have a singing quality, the smell is fragrant and the taste association is sweet. The climatic association of Earth is dampness.

Metal

Autumn is the season of Metal and represents decline. It is the period of balance between rest and activity. Metal is associated with the Lungs and Large Intestine. Its energy is about purification and elimination, about our connection with our environment, and our boundaries. Metal energy descends and disperses. The spirit of Metal is the corporeal soul, which is our animal instinct, giving us vitality and a sense of living in the here and now. Metal is associated with grief, a rotten smell and a weeping voice. The taste is aromatic or pungent. People who have a Metal imbalance are very likely to be melancholic and be overly attached to the past. The climatic association of Metal is dryness.

In health, all of the elements are found within us in equal amounts and interact harmoniously according to what is known as the Creation or Sheng cycle and Control or Ke cycle.

In the Creation cycle, each element is said to be the mother of the next, providing it with nourishment. In the Control cycle, each element will act upon another to prevent it from becoming overactive.

The Creation and Control Cycles of the Five Elements

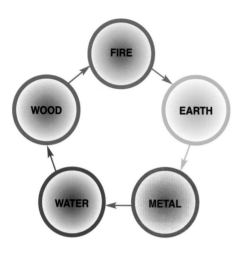

Figure 2.2: The Creation or Sheng cycle.

Wood is the child of Water and the mother of Fire. Wood creates Fire by burning.

Fire is the child of Wood and the mother of Earth. Earth is created from the ashes of Fire.

Earth is the child of Fire and mother of Metal. Earth creates Metal by hardening and producing ores.

Metal is the child of Earth and the mother of Water. Metal creates Water by melting and containment.

Water is the child of Metal and the mother of Wood. Water creates Wood by providing nourishment.

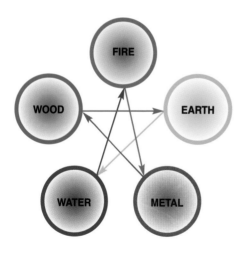

Figure 2.3: The Control or Ke cycle.

Wood controls Earth by covering and smothering.

Earth controls Water by damming.

Water controls Fire by cooling and extinguishing.

Fire controls Metal by melting.

Metal controls Wood by cutting.

A very good example of this process can be seen in the flow of a river. The river has an immense latent power able to drive turbines and carry away all in its path. However the strength of the flow is controlled by the earth banks, without which the water would flow in a random pattern with little power.

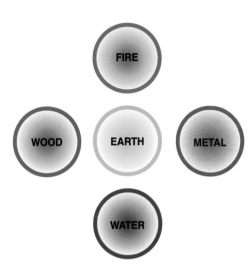

In this cycle, Water is considered to be the first Element and as such, it is the root of Yin and Yang. It is placed at the bottom and is seen as the basis of all the other elements.

Fire is placed at the top of the cycle to represent the fundamental opposites of Yin and Yang. This polarity is one of the essential ideals of Oriental medicine; i.e. the balance between the Heart and the Kidneys. Water must flow up to cool the Heart, and Fire from the Heart must descend to warm the Kidneys.

Earth is placed in the middle as the Stomach and Spleen have the principle role in the digestion of food to provide nourishment for all the other organs.

Figure 2.4: The Cosmological cycle.

The Meridians

The pathways of the meridians have been observed, mapped out and researched over thousands of years by Oriental bodyworkers, including shiatsu and tuina practitioners, acupuncturists and healers, as well as Daoist sages, Buddhist monks and martial arts practitioners. Many therapists often experience the energetic flow of Qi in their own bodies and in the body of the person they are working on. This gives them the ability to heal at a deeper level than the purely physical.

There are twelve main meridians and two extra meridians which are commonly used, although in reality there are many more. They are usually placed in a Yin-Yang pairing and if you stand in the Chinese anatomical position – with your arms raised above your head – the energy of the Yang channels will flow down towards the earth and that of the Yin channels will flow up towards the heavens. From a philosophical point of view, it is often said that 'Man stands between Heaven and Earth'. The Chinese view Man as a communion between the descending Yang energies of heaven and the ascending Yin energies of earth.

In the West, the meridians are named after their association with the major organs of the human body, although their function in Oriental medicine far exceeds those functions ascribed to organs in the Western sense.

The twelve meridian pairs are:

Lung (Lu) and Large Intestine (LI)	3am – 7am
Spleen (Sp) and Stomach (St)	7am – 11am
Heart (Ht) and Small Intestine (SI)	11am – 3pm
Kidney (Ki) and Bladder (Bl)	3pm – 7pm
Triple Heater (TH) and Heart Protector (HP)	7pm – 11pm
Liver (Lv) and Gallbladder (Gb)	11pm – 3am

The extra meridians are:

The Conception Vessel
The Governing Vessel

The energy in the main channels flows in a 24-hour cycle: and peaks in each channel for a two-hour period. Twelve hours later at the opposite end of the cycle, the energy in the channel or organ will be at its lowest point.

The Conception Vessel and the Governing Vessel have a cycle that runs up the centre line of the anterior and posterior surfaces of the torso and head, and back down through the centre of the body.

For a practitioner of shiatsu, tuina or seated acupressure bodywork, working anywhere on a meridian will have a stimulating effect on the flow of energy in these channels and will have an effect on the organs and their functions.

On the adjacent page is an illustration of the location of the main meridians on the body, with the fixed acupressure points marked by dots. Specific locations of points used in seated acupressure bodywork are dealt with later.

Lung (Lu)		Bladder (Bl)	
Large Intestine (LI)		Triple Heater (TH)	
Spleen (Sp)		Heart Protector (HP)	
Stomach (St)		Liver (Lv)	
Heart (Ht)		Gallbladder (Gb)	
Small Intestine (SI)		The Conception Vessel	
Kidney (Ki)			

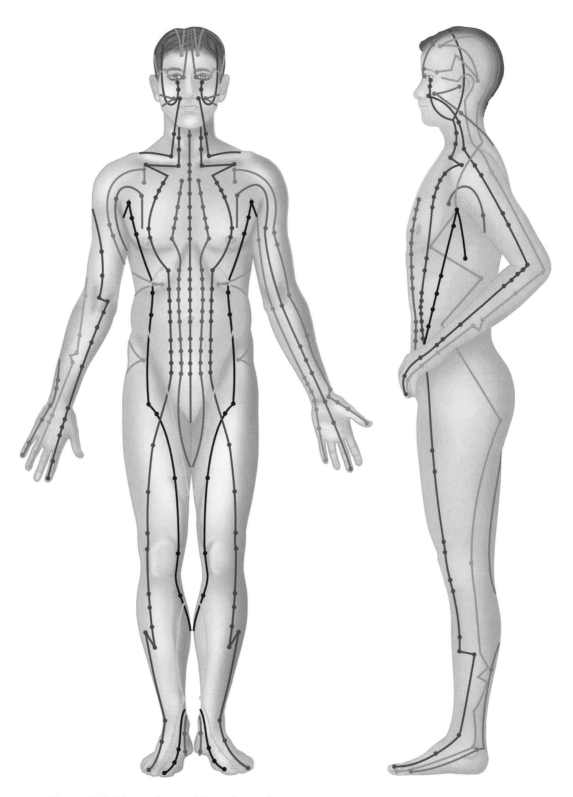

Figure 2.5: The main meridian channels.

Tsubos or Acupressure Points

If we view the meridians as a river system carrying the energy around the body, then the acupressure points or 'tsubos' can be viewed as pools where the Qi collects and becomes more easily accessible. There are about 365 main points on the channels and many extra ones not on channels. All of these points will have specific functions connected with the meridian they are on, or with its associated organ. Many of the points however have more far reaching and systemic uses, affecting not only the organs and channels but the tissues, body fluids, and even the emotions and spirit. These points are considered fixed in position, although in practice their exact location can vary. It is at these points where the energy of the meridians can be most readily affected.

There are also points known as ashi points – literally 'ouch' points – which move around and can appear anywhere on the body, both on and off the meridians.

These points are the same points that are used by acupuncturists and can be looked at as doorways into the meridian system. In fact many of the Chinese names for the points translate as door or gate, i.e. spirit gate, Qi gate, gate of hope and so on, and this can give an idea of their classical use. For those interested in knowing more, there are many excellent publications available.

Any stagnation of energy flow in the channels can create an imbalance in the body and can lead to ill-health and eventually disease. The application of positive, therapeutic and compassionate pressure to ashi points and to the acupressure points on the meridians can release blockages, tension, and accumulated stagnation in the channels, and stimulate the smooth flow of Qi, correct the functioning of the organs, and thus promote improved health.

In the seated acupressure bodywork routine it is not possible to cover all of the main acupressure points, but we are able to work effectively on several important ones, thus having an overall tonifying or stimulating effect on the body. It is beyond the scope of the seated acupressure bodyworker to treat specific ailments or illnesses, and so seated acupressure bodywork cannot be considered a remedial treatment. Therefore it is much more of a tonic or a prophylactic (preventative) treatment.

The Function of the Points

This is not intended as a book on acupressure. Therefore, for those who are interested in furthering their knowledge of this fascinating subject, there are some good books available. You may also consider studying the subject in more depth and there is a list of books and useful addresses later (*see* pp.137–140).

However, for the purposes of this book it is useful to understand and be aware of the function of a few of the main points which you will use during seated acupressure bodywork. The following pages give an overview of the channels you will be contacting during your Kata and the major points on those channels.

Small Intestine Meridian

The Qi of the Small Intestine meridian provides a sense of balance, rhythm and contentment when flowing smoothly.

Function: Assimilation, separation of pure from impure, absorption of fluids.

Affects: Abdomen, passage of food, absorption, mental discrimination, the ability to sort information and make decisions.

Point	Location	Function
Small Intestine 3	Located on the ulnar side of the hand distal to the head of the 5th metacarpal, about midway between the little finger joint and wrist joint	Good for digestive complaints and abdominal pains. Good point for releasing the neck

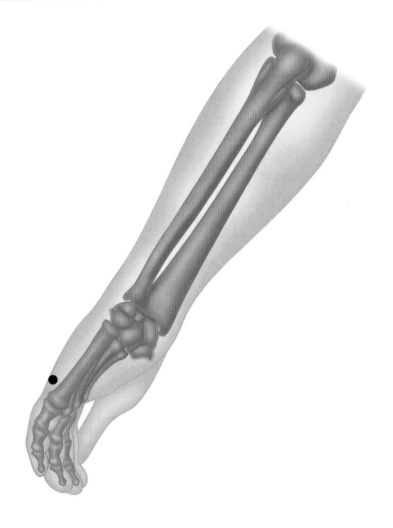

Figure 2.6: The main point on the Small Intestine meridian.

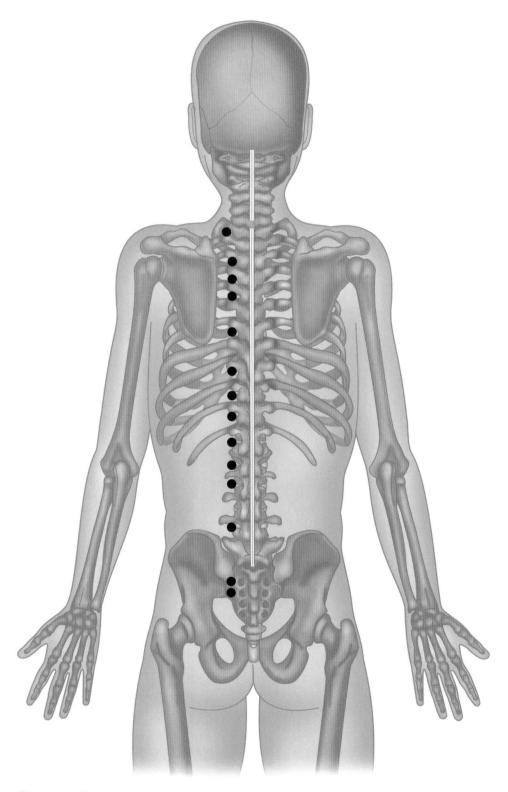

Figure 2.7: The main points on the Bladder meridian.

Bladder Meridian

Function: Purification, elimination, storage and excretion of urine.
Affects: The urinary system, the autonomic nervous system, bones,
                     teeth, hair, ears, the spinal column and water metabolism.
                     Gives a person courage.

The Bladder meridian has two lines running down either side of the spine and is the one with which you will have most contact. Along this meridian are a series of points called Yu points (Japanese), Shu points (Chinese) or Back Transporting points. Each of these points is named after and associated with one of the Internal Organs, and has a direct affect on its function and therefore on the channel of the same name.

Skilled bodywork practitioners are able to diagnose a client's condition by connecting with these points and by the feel of the Bladder meridian as it passes along the spinal column. Working the Bladder meridian will balance and tonify the whole system as well as having a slightly eliminating effect on the client.

All these points on the Bladder meridian have a direct action on the energy of the organ after which they are named and are located on the back, 1.5 cun lateral to the centre line, at the level of the lower border of the spinous processes of the vertebrae.

Point	Location	Function
Bladder 11	1.5 cun lateral to the gap between T1 & T2	Point for bones
Bladder 13	1.5 cun lateral to the gap between T3 & T4	Lung point
Bladder 14	1.5 cun lateral to the gap between T4 & T5	Heart Protector point
Bladder 15	1.5 cun lateral to the gap between T5 & T6	Heart point
Bladder 17	1.5 cun lateral to the gap between T7 & T8	Hiccup (Diaphragm) point
Bladder 18	1.5 cun lateral to the gap between T9 & T10	Liver point
Bladder 19	1.5 cun lateral to the gap between T10 & T11	Gallbladder point
Bladder 20	1.5 cun lateral to the gap between T11 & T12	Spleen point
Bladder 21	1.5 cun lateral to the gap between T12 & L1	Stomach point
Bladder 22	1.5 cun lateral to the gap between L1 & L2	Triple Heater point
Bladder 23	1.5 cun lateral to the gap between L2 & L3	Kidney point
Bladder 25	1.5 cun lateral to the gap between L4 & L5	Large Intestine point
Bladder 27	1.5 cun lateral to the centre line above the 1st sacral foramen	Bladder point
Bladder 28	1.5 cun lateral to the centre line above the 2nd sacral foramen	Small Intestine point

Large Intestine Meridian

The Qi of the Large Intestine meridian is good for keeping things moving. When the Qi does not flow in this channel, people may become withdrawn.

Function: Elimination and excretion. Vitality.

Affects: Bowels, skin, nose, sinuses, self-confidence, ability to let go.

Point	Location	Function
Large Intestine 4	Located at the midpoint of the second metacarpal. Press the highest point of the fleshy mound between the thumb and index finger	Good for headaches, toothache, constipation, neck problems and sinus problems. Contraindicated in pregnancy
Large Intestine 10	Located on the radial side of the dorsal surface of the forearm, three fingers or 2 cun distal to the cubital crease on a line between LI5 and LI11	Tonifies the Qi and blood
Large Intestine 11	Located at the lateral end of the elbow crease when the elbow is held at a 90° angle	Arm pains (tennis elbow), headaches, diarrhoea, fevers

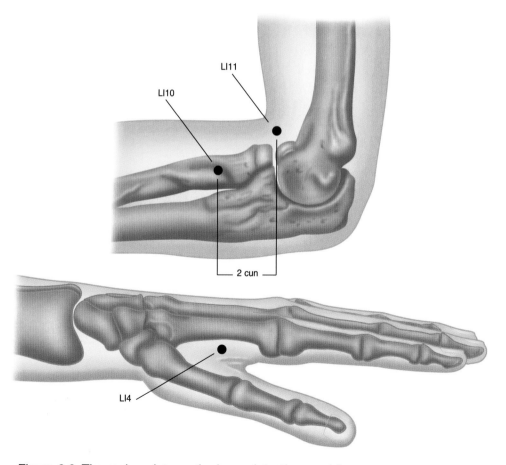

Figure 2.8: The main points on the Large Intestine meridian.

Gallbladder Meridian

The Qi of this meridian helps the smooth flow of energy all around the system.

Function: Aids digestion, smooths the flow of Qi, assists in decision making.

Affects: The digestive system, the flanks or sides of the body, the ligaments and tendons.

Point	Location	Function
Gallbladder 20	Located on the occipital border, in the depression between the sternocleidomastoideus and trapezius muscles	Good for spasms, neck pains and headaches
Gallbladder 21	Midway between the centre line of the back at the level of C7/T1 and the acromion process, at the highest point of the shoulder	Good for shoulder and neck pain, contraindicated in pregnancy

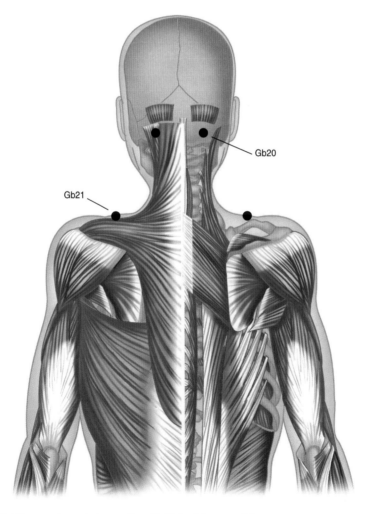

Figure 2.9: The main points on the Gallbladder meridian.

Triple Heater Meridian

The Qi of the Triple Heater meridian regulates our body temperature.

Function: Protection. Harmonizes the upper, middle and lower sections of
                       the torso. Creates and distributes warmth around the body via the
                       meridian system.

Affects: The immune system, social interaction and emotional protection and
                       the body's thermostat.

Point	Location	Function
Triple Heater 4	On the transverse crease of the dorsum of the wrist, in the depression ulnar to the tendon of muscle extensor digitorum communis	Good for pain, swelling and loss of mobility of the hand, wrist and elbow. Clears heat from the body and so is good for inflammatory conditions such as headaches, tonsillitis, thirst and inflammatory ear problems
Triple Heater 5	2 cun or 3 finger widths proximal to Triple Heater 4, between the radius and the ulna	This is a very powerful point for the treatment of colds and flu, chills and fevers, sore throats, headaches and pain and stiffness of the neck and shoulders

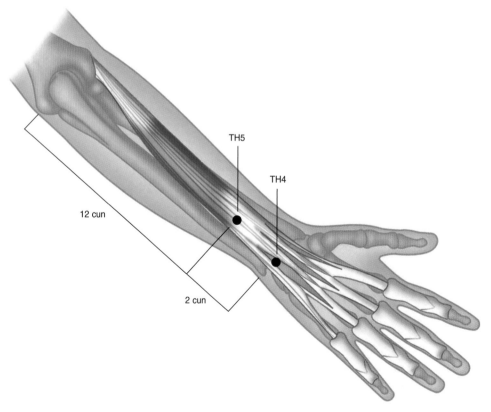

TH5

TH4

12 cun

2 cun

Figure 2.10: The main points on the Triple Heater meridian.

Heart Meridian

The Qi of the Heart meridian provides a sense of self and is responsible for our consciousness.

Function: Provides a sense of rhythm and coordination: when out of balance can lead to anxiety and panic attacks.

Affects: Sleep patterns, the cardiovascular system and the nervous system.

Point	Location	Function
Heart 7	At the ulnar end of the wrist crease, in a hollow just radial to the pisiform bone	Good for hysteria, insomnia, anxiety, panic attacks

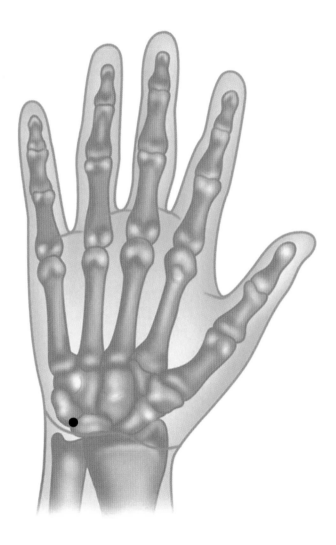

Figure 2.11: The main point on the Heart meridian.

Heart Protector Meridian

The Qi of this meridian when stimulated has a very calming effect and is good for stress.

Function: Protects the Heart, benefits circulation.

Affects: The Heart, veins and arteries, blood, our emotions and our
                       relationships with others.

Point	Location	Function
Heart Protector 6	Located on the anterior surface of the forearm, between the two tendons of flexor carpi radialis and palmaris longus, about 3 finger widths proximal to the wrist crease	Good for anxiety attacks, morning sickness and motion sickness
Heart Protector 8	Located in the centre of the palm at the point where the middle finger touches when a loose fist is made	Good for stress relief, overwork, and helps improve blood circulation

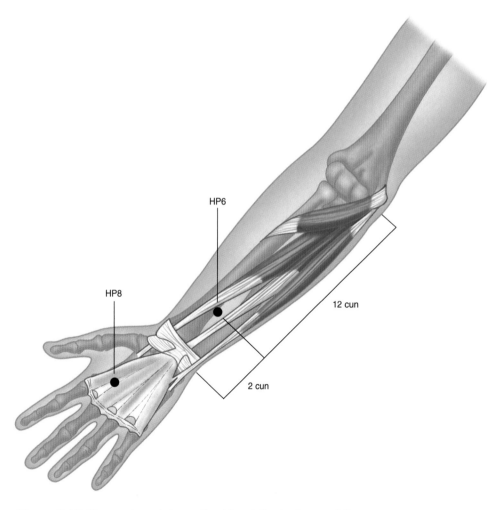

Figure 2.12: The main points on the Heart Protector meridian.

Lung Meridian

The Qi of this meridian is good for physical endurance and positive thinking. When not flowing smoothly we are likely to feel depressed.

Function: Intake of Qi from the air. Vitality.

Affects: Lungs, nose, skin, breathing, sinuses, mental vitality, and positive outlook.

Point	Location	Function
Lung 5	In the hollow just lateral to the biceps brachii tendon in the centre of the elbow crease	Good for sore throats, coughs and colds
Lung 7	Approximately 3 finger widths proximal to the wrist crease on the radial edge of the forearm, where the skin changes colour	Good for coughs, cold and asthma

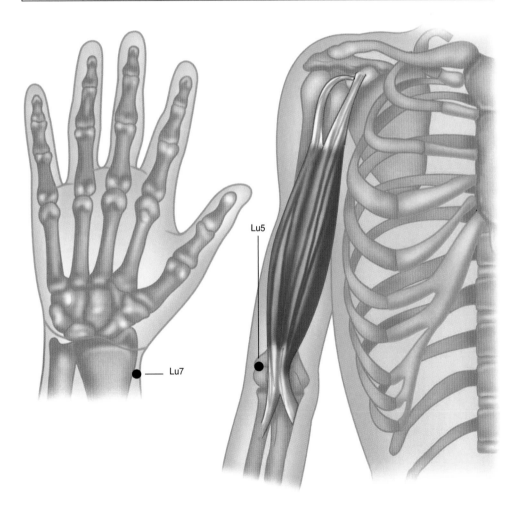

Figure 2.13: The main points on the Lung meridian.

CHAPTER 3

Stress in the Workplace

In May 2004 the BUPA health information team published a report estimating that over six million working days were lost to work-related stress, linking stress as a causative factor in many illnesses, both minor and major.

For the majority of us, work is a significant part of our lives. Many of us may spend around 25% of our adult lives working. It provides not only a regular income and therefore spending ability, but also gives structure to our lives, giving us a sense of purpose and satisfaction. Our workplace however can also be a major source of stress and worry.

Why Does Stress Occur?

Stress is a natural response in the body as it prepares us to face a threat: whether real or perceived. During stress, the balance between the sympathetic (prepares body systems during emergency situations) and parasympathetic (conserves energy, promotes relaxation, rest and repair) nervous systems is overridden. Situations or stimuli, known as *stressors*, trigger certain responses. Stressors can be acute, causing short-lived effects, or chronic, causing long-term changes to the body.

The hypothalamus-pituitary-adrenal (HPA) axis part of the stress response begins with the release of a hormone called *adrenocorticotrophic hormone* (ACTH) from the pituitary gland to the adrenal cortex, which leads to an instant release of natural chemicals into the system, such as adrenaline, noradrenaline, and corticosteroids, e.g. cortisol. The corticosteroids enable more energy to be released into the body for the fight-or-flight response, by facilitating the conversion of protein and fat stores into glucose. Consequently, the heart beats faster, the respiratory rate increases, blood pressure rises and other body systems like the digestive system react as well. The fight-or-flight response, first described by Walter Cannon in 1929, is a very effective way of dealing with a physical threat. An animal has two options when faced with danger. They can either face the threat ('fight'), or they can avoid the threat ('flight').

If the stressor is removed, the physiological activity in the body gradually returns to normal. The adrenal glands stop pumping out hormones, sympathetic nervous system activity decreases, and parasympathetic activity resumes. However, problems occur if the body prepares to face the threat or problem, but no action is taken to resolve it. This is because the body's systems remain over stimulated. If this happens repeatedly the system becomes frustrated and overloaded, leading to what are commonly called the symptoms of stress. The correct term is a 'negative stress' response.

Another situation that can cause a negative stress response occurs when many minor problems occur on a regular and repetitive daily basis, eventually cumulating to cause the symptoms of stress. These minor stressful experiences can include balancing the demands of work, home, partners and children, fitting everything into a 24-hour day and keeping them all happy. In a situation like this, our fight-or-flight response can be triggered continually, but without being successfully resolved. There is then a very real possibility that people will respond to the stress by starting to drink heavily, taking drugs, excessive smoking, or by eventually becoming ill.

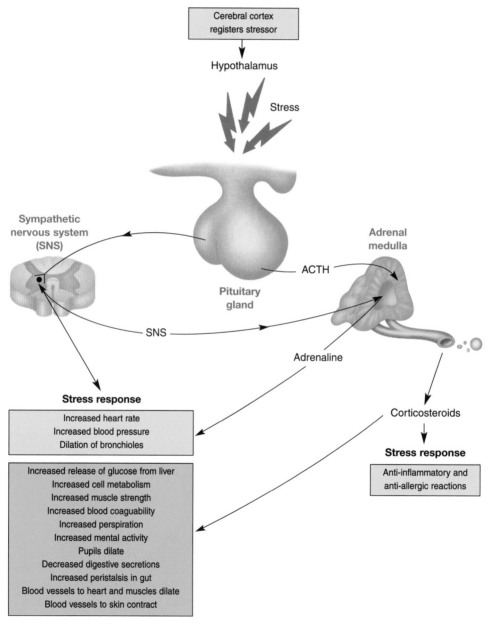

Figure 3.1: The responses by the body systems to the 'fight-or-flight' response.

It isn't easy to find a generally acceptable definition of 'stress'. *Dorland's Illustrated Medical Dictionary* defines it as: "a state of physiological or psychological strain caused by adverse stimuli, physical, mental, or emotional, internal or external, that tend to disturb the functioning of an organism and which the organism naturally desires to avoid."

The Holmes-Rahe Social Adjustment Scale

Any change in the routine of our lives – even welcome ones – can be stressful, both in terms of the way in which we perceive them and in terms of the increased incidence of physical illness and death that occur during the following 12 months. The Holmes-Rahe Scale assigns values (based upon the sample being told that marriage represents 50 points) attributed by a sample of 394 individuals to the life events concerned.

Events	Scale of Impact	Events	Scale of Impact
Death of spouse	100	Foreclosure of mortgage or loan	30
Divorce	75	Change in responsibilities at work	29
Marital separation	65	Son or daughter leaving home	29
Jail term	63	Trouble with in-laws	29
Death of a close family member	63	Outstanding personal achievement	28
Personal injury or illness	53	Partner begins or stops work	26
Marriage	50	Begin or end school	26
Dismissal from work	47	Change in living conditions	25
Marital reconciliation	45	Revision of personal habits	24
Retirement	45	Trouble with boss	23
Change in health of family member	44	Change in work hours or conditions	20
Pregnancy	40	Change in residence/schools/recreation	19
Sex difficulties	39	Change in social activities	18
Gain of new family member	39	Small mortgage or loan	17
Business readjustment	39	Change in sleeping/eating habits	16
Change in financial state	38	Change in no. of family get-togethers	15
Death of close friend	37	Vacation	13
Change to different line of work	36	Christmas	12
Change in no. of arguments with spouse	36	Minor violations of the law	11
Major mortgage	31		

Don't attempt to add up a 'score' on this scale. The values are there simply to show the relative impact of stressful events and to give some indication of the wide range of stressors in our lives. And the list is by no means complete. Most people can add items to it, many of them likely to carry high values. *Source: Managing Stress*, The British Psychology Society, David Fontana, 1989.

What is Work-related Stress?

There will always be a certain amount of pressure surrounding our working lives, such as deadlines to meet, budgets to be kept, demanding employers, or rivalry and unfriendliness between colleagues. A certain amount of external pressure is actually a necessary stimulus, triggering the fight-or-flight response of our hormonal system. Some people actually thrive with this added short-term pressure, thinking more clearly and becoming more productive. The human body is designed to respond to these short-term demands. It releases hormones such as adrenaline into our system, raising our heart rate and increasing respiration, thus preparing us for action. However prolonged and excessive periods of stress will eventually take their toll on our health and can produce a wide range of both physical and emotional symptoms.

Work-related stress is usually the result of an accumulation of stressful factors occurring over a period of time rather than being the response to a single stimulus or problem. It can also be triggered by sudden and unexpected pressure. The most common causes of stress at work are related to management and organizational issues, relationships at work and your own sense of being in control of your workplace.

Everyone will experience stress in different ways. Some people will feel the effects more than others and some people will become so used to the symptoms of excessive stress that they do not notice the detrimental results on their health. How you respond will depend largely on your personality and how you respond to pressure. Therefore, what is a stressful experience for one person may not be for another. The 2004 BUPA report identified the following triggers for stress:

- Lack of control over work;
- Excessive time pressures;
- Inflexible or long working hours;
- Too much or too little work or responsibility;
- Confusion about duties and responsibilities;
- Lack of job variety and interest;
- Inadequate training and possibilities for learning new skills;
- Poor balance between work and life away from work;
- Difficult relationships at work;
- Lack of support and lack of contact with colleagues;
- Organisational confusion, restructuring, job change;
- Uncertainty over job prospects.

Symptoms of Work-related Stress

Work-related stress can produce problems with both physical and emotional health and may affect behavioural patterns at work and at home. Physical symptoms might include:

- Increased susceptibility to colds or infections;
- Headaches;
- Muscular tension;
- Backache and neck ache;
- Excessive tiredness;
- Difficulty sleeping;
- Digestive problems;
- Raised heart rate;
- Increased sweating;
- Lower sex drive;
- Skin rashes;
- Blurred vision.

Emotional and behavioural changes due to work-related stress might include:

- Wanting to cry much of the time;
- Feeling that you can't cope;
- A short temper at work and at home;
- Feeling that you've achieved nothing at the end of the day;
- Eating when you're not hungry;
- Loss of appetite;
- Smoking and drinking to get you through the day;
- Inability to plan, concentrate and control work;
- Getting less work done;
- Poor relationships with colleagues or clients;
- Loss of motivation and commitment.

Disorders of the Upper Limb

The Health and Safety Executive (HSE) uses the term 'upper limb disorders' (ULDs) to replace 'repetitive strain injuries' (RSI). ULDs are often caused by work-related activity such as typing, and in these cases they are termed WRULDs (work-related upper limb disorders). Type I ULDs are caused by a specific condition, such as tendonitis or tenosynovitis. Type II ULDs are caused by no specific condition. It is estimated that 4.1 million working days (full-day equivalent) were lost in 2001/02 through musculo-skeletal disorders which were caused or made worse by work. On average, each person suffering took an estimated 17.8 days off in that 12-month period.

Self-help

It is virtually impossible to completely avoid stressful situations and pressure at work, so it is therefore important to learn how to manage the stress as it occurs. There are a number of very effective ways of reducing the negative impact of stress. It is important to deal with the problem as soon as possible and one of the best methods is effective time management.

- Prioritize tasks;
- Delegate where necessary;
- Do not take on more than you can handle;
- Complete one task before going on to the next.

Make time to relax at work by taking regular short breaks, stretching and breathing deeply. This will help you to keep focused and prevent tired muscles. Make sure you get outside for a walk or some fresh air during your lunch or coffee breaks.

Changing Your Lifestyle

Participating in regular activities away from work will take your mind away from work worries and remind you that there is life outside the office. Learn a new skill, start a new hobby or take up a new sport: this will bring a new sense of purpose into your life and help you meet new friends.

There is increasing evidence that participating in a regular physical activity not only helps to reduce stress levels, but also improves sleep and enhances general energy levels. It provides valuable 'time out' and can trigger chemicals in the brain that improve mood. Taking a brisk walk every day, walking to work instead of sitting in the car for example, would be ideal. It is however important that you choose some form of physical activity that you enjoy, such as golf, cycling, swimming and dancing.

Learning how to relax may improve sleep and may help to relieve physical problems such as headaches, indigestion, bloating and so on, which more often than not are as a result of stress. Talking to and confiding in close friends or relatives is a good way to express your worries and negativity. Sharing your problems can help to give you a new perspective, which in itself can minimize stress.

Try to eat a balanced, high-fibre diet and regular meals, which will help you to maintain stable energy levels throughout the day. Try to avoid resorting to stimulants like coffee, alcohol and excessive smoking or recreational drugs as an escape from your problems. These will increase stress levels and inevitably lead to a 'low' when their effects wear off.

Take time at the end of every day to reflect on what you have achieved and remember that tomorrow is a new day. Try not to worry about what the future holds and take each day as it comes.

Seeking Further Help

Occasionally work-related stress may turn into a long-term problem and people will need to seek further help, as they may become depressed or suffer from anxiety. If you become concerned about yourself or a colleague, contact your GP who can either treat you or refer you on for a more specialist treatment. It may be recommended that you attend a stress management course or need to contact a confidential counseling service. Your local library, health centre or the social services will have details of local resources.

Without any doubt, we will experience stress at many points throughout our lives and in particular at work. However, if we were to go through life without any pressures or challenges we would merely exist from day-to-day, and our lives would lack vitality and excitement, both at home and at work. We all require some stress to give our lives a certain spark. But every one of us can at any time become overwhelmed by stress, particularly those of us who lead very busy and high maintenance lifestyles, and suffer the exhausting effects it can have. There are many ways of managing our stress levels, and every one of us should make it our goal to discover our own very personal way and organize our lives accordingly.

Seated Acupressure Bodywork and Stress Management

Whilst by no means being the complete or perfect answer to stress management, any form of bodywork can work to effectively relax, calm and return harmony and homeostatic balance to the human body. This direct response to the negative stress response is as effective as the fight-or-flight response. However, long-term stress management plans will still be necessary to prevent a recurring problem. Seated acupressure bodywork received regularly at your place of work can be a very effective first step to a relatively stress free life.

CHAPTER 4

Screening Clients and Contraindications to Seated Acupressure Bodywork

It is essential to always screen your clients for any contraindications, even if giving very short treatments, for example at a health fair or demonstration. In some situations, a short verbal screening is considered to be sufficient. For example, in one group of back rub shops, a laminated sheet is shown to clients asking them to declare any health issues they may have and thus take responsibility for their own health. It is important to ensure that you comply with any requirements set down by your insurance company as to how you keep records. I would suggest that when working privately, you obtain a written declaration of a client's health and suitability before the first treatment. An example of a screening form is shown on page 119. A shorter version has been included for use at public events. Note that it is very important to reassure the client that this information will be held in the strictest confidence.

Screening Forms

The use of a screening form is helpful in several ways:

- It saves time because a client can be filling in the form whilst you are working on someone else;
- Once the client has completed the form, you can very quickly ascertain what other questions you may need to ask;
- It gives the client a certain amount of anonymity in a public space, because it minimizes the need for them to verbalize their answers to sensitive questions;
- It enables you to keep records of everyone who you treat.

It is however still very important that you converse with your client.

Observation

Visual screening is also very important. Clients are well known for not telling their practitioner everything. For example, they may not actually be aware of the effect their medication is having on them. People who have had too much to drink or who have been taking recreational drugs may not tell you. If anyone appears to be too unwell for treatment, you need to take this into account.

Explaining the Procedure and Getting Feedback

Always explain to a new client what to expect from the treatment. Explain how to sit on the chair, the sort of techniques you are likely to use, and how long it will take. Explain to them about the effects of pressure on their muscular system, and about not resisting the pressure you will apply. Explain how to use their out-breath to relax their muscles as you apply the pressure to particular points, or on stretches.

Ask if they have had bodywork before and what sort of pressure they like. If they have never had any form of bodywork or massage it is important to check at several points throughout the sequence that the pressure is alright, and that you are not applying either too much or too little.

Keeping Records

I thoroughly recommend keeping brief records of all treatments. Not only do they act as a reminder of each client's particular likes and dislikes, but also allow you to record responses to the treatment and how the client felt afterwards. Keeping records also enables you to provide evidence that a proper screening was carried out before the treatment.

Things to Consider Before Each Backrub

The comfort of your client is very important:

- Ensure that their knees are correctly positioned on the chair and are far enough forward;
- Check that there is no lordosis or arching of their lower back;
- If you are using a standard chair or a stool, ensure the client's knees are in front of their feet;
- Ask if the pressure is all right, i.e. not too much or too little, when working with the elbow or thumbs down the nine points on the upper and lower back;
- When in doubt, do not proceed: always err on the side of caution.

Pay attention to your posture:

- Ensure you keep your back straight and your feet apart. When you bend, bend at the hips rather than the waist, and move your body in the direction of the pressure you are applying;
- Keep your centre of gravity and energy low, and initiate all movements from the Hara (lower abdomen);
- Try to keep your hips at right angles to the direction of movement, with one foot behind the other;
- Keep the front leg bent and the back leg straight;
- 'Squiggle' back on the ball of your foot as you move down the back, to maintain your posture and a 90° angle.

Pay attention to your technique:

- Apply perpendicular pressure, i.e. at a 90° angle to the plane of the body you are working on;
- Keep your arms straight, i.e. shoulder behind your elbow and elbow behind your hand or thumbs;
- Try to maintain a 90° angle at the shoulder;
- Apply the pressure evenly and steadily, and release in a similar fashion;
- Release the pressure but not the contact when moving around the body. Try to maintain a two-handed contact at all times;
- Be careful not to jab or poke. It is extremely uncomfortable to have an uncontrolled elbow pressing into the back;
- Don't forget to breathe as naturally as possible.

Intention is all-important:

- Your intention is important. You will never give a good backrub if your mind is elsewhere;
- Relax and allow the sequence to flow;
- Learn the sequence well and it will do the work for you;
- Enjoy the interaction and energetic exchange between you and your client;
- Experience the dance. Enjoy the experience yourself, then both you and your client will benefit more.

Contraindications to Seated Acupressure Bodywork (includes Special Care Conditions)

The contraindications to seated acupressure bodywork are essentially the same as for any bodywork system that works on the major muscle groups of the body. The main differences are the upright posture of the receiver and the more energetic and dispersive techniques that are used.

- High or low blood pressure – People with high or low blood pressure may feel light-headed when they sit up. Acupressure bodywork may lower blood pressure, so be careful with people on medication.
- History of fainting – Low blood sugar or low blood pressure. Make sure they have eaten earlier in the day.
- Avoid heavy work on the lower back if they have just had a large meal.
- Avoid areas such as fractures, dislocations, and recent injections.
- Do not work on people under the influence of recreational drugs or alcohol.
- Avoid working on people who have had recent surgery or are recovering from a serious illness.
- Pregnant women or women who are trying to conceive should not receive any acupressure work. Modify the routine to include table massage work, effleurage over the back, neck, arms, and especially the head (*see* page 108).

- Skin conditions such as psoriasis or eczema are not contraindications unless there is broken skin. Just avoid applying any friction and avoid the affected area. Avoid working on areas of infected skin.
- Do not work on anyone who has suffered a trauma or injury in the last 24 hours.
- Do not work on anyone who has a communicable disease, e.g. influenza.

People with the following complaints should ideally get consent from their GP prior to treatment:

- Arthritis;
- Cancer;
- Diabetes;
- Epilepsy;
- Long-term medication;

- Osteoarthritis;
- Osteoporosis;
- Rheumatism;
- Thrombosis;
- Shoulder or hip replacements.

If in doubt don't do it!

If a client should faint or feel faint, place them in the recovery position or sit them with their head between their knees and give them a glass of water. Do not leave them whilst they are feeling unwell and try to find out why they may have fainted; i.e. history of fainting, empty stomach, blood pressure problems, medication, recent illness, etc.

More on Contraindications

Acute illness or fever
Massage is contraindicated. Where a client is suffering from a cold but is otherwise in good health, it is possible to work on them, but advise them that the treatment may make their symptoms worse in the short-term.

Alcohol / recreational drugs
It is advisable not to treat anyone under the influence of these substances.

Acute musculo-skeletal problems
Avoid working on the affected area and refer the client on to a specialist in this area (e.g. physiotherapist, chiropractor, etc.).

Arthritis
Determine the location, severity and type of arthritis, and how long they have had it. Also determine whether it is a 'hot' or 'cold' type arthritis. If it is hot, avoid working the inflamed areas. In all other cases avoid vigorous techniques and work within the client's comfort zone. Be very careful with stretches and techniques such as finger snaps. If your client has arthritis in the knees show them how to sit with their legs outstretched.

Broken bones
Work no lower than one joint above the break. After the bone has healed, work with caution over the area.

Bruising
Avoid working over areas of recent or heavy bruising.

Cancer
Massage is not contraindicated in certain types of cancer, but it is advisable to obtain permission from the client's medical practitioner before commencing treatment.

Diabetes
Check with the client what type of treatment they are having. It is important to avoid recent injection sites. Ensure that the client's blood sugar levels are stable and inform them that seated acupressure bodywork can have a similar effect to exercise. Suggest that they monitor their blood sugar levels after the massage. Check if they are prone to bruising, or if they have any loss of sensation or numbness in their extremities.

Epilepsy
Determine how stable their epilepsy is, how long they have been diagnosed, how long they have been on medication, and when their last seizure was. If they are still very unstable, seated acupressure bodywork is contraindicated. Check that the client is aware of the stimuli that precede an attack, and if they are comfortable with you working around their neck and head. If they are not, avoid working these areas.

Heart disease
Establish the type of disease and its severity. In the case of a recent heart attack or a recent disease, modify your treatment to exclude any techniques that will over-stimulate the client. Remember, you can always alter the format of your routine and use gentler, less stimulating techniques. You may wish to get the client's medical practitioners' consent.

High blood pressure
Establish if any medication is being taken and check that they are aware of any side effects that may occur. Ask if the blood pressure is stable and if they experience any symptoms. It is important to be aware that this type of massage can lower the blood pressure. Be particularly careful when working around the neck and on the inner arms.

Low blood pressure
Determine how and if their blood pressure affects them. Be aware that many people with low blood pressure will exhibit no symptoms. Remember that seated acupressure bodywork can lower the blood pressure. Be particularly careful if they experience regular or prolonged periods of dizziness or feeling faint. Be careful when working around the neck and inner arm.

Low blood sugar
It is important that your client has eaten within the last 2 to 3 hours.

Osteoporosis
Osteoporosis causes a thinning and weakening of the bone structure, so it is important to determine the location and severity of the problem. Avoid working over the affected areas, and use caution with techniques such as elbow press or palm press.

Record Keeping

It is very important to maintain adequate records about your clients and to reassure the client that these records are confidential. Create a screening questionnaire (*see* page 119) for the first time you see someone. Check that there are no contraindications to having this sort of massage before the first treatment, and then keep records each time you see someone. It is important to keep track of any positive or negative reactions your clients may have.

Obviously in some situations, i.e. shops or exhibitions, it is not always possible to take full details from someone, so a shorter version is possible. In some places you may just conduct a verbal screening of your clients. With experience, you will learn to evaluate what level of screening is appropriate to the situation but the ultimate responsibility lies with you.

Create a schedule of appointments and try to stay on schedule. Do not forget to build in breaks for yourself.

Looking After Yourself – Personal Care

As a seated acupressure bodyworker it is very important that you look after your own health and wellbeing. It is all too easy especially if you are working in a busy environment to forget to take breaks, eat lunch, etc. I personally would recommend that you take a break every two hours. A thirty-minute break would be ideal. If you are self-employed and find your own customers, this is easy as you can make a contract with them and write a rest period into your working day. But obviously if you are only doing two hours, this does not apply.

If you decide to work for a seated acupressure bodywork company, check out their terms of employment and ensure that you are entitled to a sufficient number of rest periods in your day. Seven or eight hours of constant massage is very tiring on both your hands and feet as well as on an emotional level.

I would also recommend that you do some sort of warming up exercises or stretching before starting work, to loosen up your joints and warm your muscles (*see* pp.103–106). Qigong exercises are very good for this, as they not only help to warm up and focus the body, but they work on an emotional level as well, helping to keep you focused and grounded.

A Word on Hygiene

- You will be seeing a lot of people in the course of your day and it is very important that you maintain high standards of hygiene for yourself, your equipment, and in your working environment;
- Wear clean, fresh clothes because you will be working very closely with people, and the smell of stale clothing is not pleasant;
- Ensure you keep your fingernails clean and short;
- Do not wear strong perfume or aftershave. Some people may have an allergic reaction to these or just find them objectionable;
- Eat only on breaks;

- Wash your hands or clean them with a wet wipe between each client;
- Cover any open cuts with a waterproof plaster;
- Do not work if you have a cold, cough or any other contagious illness;
- Wipe the chair, especially the face cradle with a sterile wipe between each client;
- Cover the face cradle with a clean cover or tissue for each new client;
- Ensure that all of your equipment is well maintained and in good working order.

Preparing your Client for Seated Acupressure Bodywork

Many of your prospective clients may never have considered having a massage before. Many people are put off by the thought of undressing in front of a stranger and even more so by the thought of being touched by one. It is therefore very important how you present yourself as a practitioner, as this may well be their first experience of any form of bodywork.

With seated acupressure bodywork, it is very possible that your client will have just come from a very stressful and demanding environment and may be worried or nervous about their first appointment. Be aware of the impact your language, both spoken and body language, will have on them. If necessary, reassure them that seated acupressure bodywork is an enjoyable experience and not in the least painful. Explain to your client what to expect from a session and ask them a few questions to decide if the massage is appropriate. If you have not already done so, explain to them what seated acupressure bodywork can do for them. Leaflets and flyers are useful for this.

Explain that seated acupressure bodywork can have some or all of the following effects.

- Promotes a sense of wellbeing;
- Unravels tense and aching muscles;
- Stretches cramped muscles, tendons and ligaments;
- Relieves minor aches and pains;
- Encourages a state of alert relaxation;
- Allows the body's life energy (or Qi) to flow more freely;
- Soothes and balances the nervous system;
- Increases the circulation to the whole body, but especially the back, neck, head, arms, and shoulders;
- Is an immediate stress-buster;
- Can help prevent minor conditions becoming more serious if used regularly;
- And most importantly, it feels great.

More on Client Preparation

It is very important to do the following in front of the client every time you see them:

- Clean the face cushion with a wet wipe;
- Wash or wipe your hands with a wet wipe;
- Towel-dry the face cushion and your hands;
- Place a fresh disposable face cover or tissue on the face cushion and create an appropriate breathing hole;
- Before seating your client, ask them to remove their coat and hang it nearby;

- Recommend the loosening of ties, neck scarves and shirt collars;
- Ask if they would remove any jewellery that may get in the way, and put it somewhere safe;
- Ensure they have turned off any mobile telephones;
- If it is their first massage, demonstrate how to sit on the chair, and help them onto the chair if necessary;
- Adjust the face cushion, arm rest and chest pad to ensure they are comfortable;
- Ensure that their head is not tilted backwards compressing the vertebrae of the neck, adjusting the angle of the head rest if necessary;
- Check that their lower back is not arched or curved;
- Ask them to tell you immediately if they would like more or less pressure at any time and to let you know if anything is painful or uncomfortable;
- Ensure that no part of them is pressing against any hard part of the chair;
- Lastly, tell them to simply lean forwards, relax into the support of the chair and enjoy the experience.

Getting Started

The equipment needed to get started as a seated acupressure bodyworker is minimal, and if you are moving around from office to office, the less you carry the better.

The essential equipment:

- A seated acupressure bodywork chair or desktop system;
- Sanitizer for the face support and the hands;
- Disposable covers or tissues for the face cradle;
- Scissors.

When travelling to a client's place of work, you may wish to take a CD player and appropriate music with you as this can help create an air of calm in the office. In some places it can be useful to have water on hand to offer your clients after treatment. It is particularly important to offer water or advise having a drink after a long session.

When travelling to offices, it is also important to take your own 'office' with you, which should include:

- Diary or appointment book and pen;
- Appointment cards;
- Client screening sheets;
- Client treatment records;
- Gift vouchers and / or loyalty or discount cards;
- Receipt books;
- Change (for cash clients).

Promotional Material

- Business cards;
- Leaflets and flyers;
- Posters;
- Educational information (this can include literature on healthy lifestyles, exercise, stress relief, etc.);
- Press articles and magazine items, especially local news items.

When working at exhibitions and shows, you may also find it useful to have:

- Large posters;
- Pictures of people receiving seated acupressure bodywork;
- Price lists;
- A display board and spotlights;
- Video or PowerPoint display;
- Water and refreshments;
- Rubbish bin.

BLACKPOOL & FYLDE
ANSDELL
RESOURCE
CENTRE
COLLEGE

CHAPTER 6

The 20-Minute Seated Acupressure Bodywork Sequence

A Word on Posture

Throughout this form, posture and body position are important in order that you can apply the best pressure without unduly straining yourself. It is important to be directly opposite and facing the area that you are working on, and to apply pressure by dropping your body weight rather than using muscular strength.

At all times try to maintain an erect posture without undue twist: this way you will avoid backache. Try to keep your hips facing at right angles to the direction of your movement and the pressure you are applying. Make sure you are feeling calm and relaxed and well grounded, and that all techniques are applied with perpendicular pressure. The basic posture we use is similar to that of a martial arts practitioner.

Stand with your feet about two shoulder widths apart, one behind the other in a lunge position. The front knee should be bent with the knee above the heel and the back leg should be straight. About 60%–70% of your body weight should be on your front leg. Your hips should be turned to the front. It is important to always have your back leg directly behind the area on which you are working to allow a good transmission of body weight rather than the use of upper body strength to apply pressure. This means that if you are working down one side of the spine, you will need to step slightly to one side of the chair.

- Keep your back straight and your centre of gravity low, moving with your lower body and not your upper body;
- Keep one foot in front of the other with the rear one in line with the direction of applied pressure;
- Keep the front knee flexed and the back leg straight. The front foot should be in front of the knee;
- Keep the back heel off the floor as this will help you to move more efficiently;
- Do not use muscular strength to apply pressure but ensure you are in the correct position to drop your body weight into the point or channel;
- Do not be tempted to drop or dip your hips as you apply pressure;
- Ensure your arms are always perpendicular to the part of the body where you are applying pressure;
- Always try to maintain a right angle between your upper arm and your body and try to keep your arms straight, with your shoulders, elbows, and wrists in line;
- Always 'squiggle' with your back foot to maintain your position as you move down the back from point to point.

Keep your back straight and your centre of gravity low

Always try to maintain a right angle between your upper arm and body and try to keep your arms straight

Ensure that your arms are always perpendicular to the part of the body where you are applying pressure

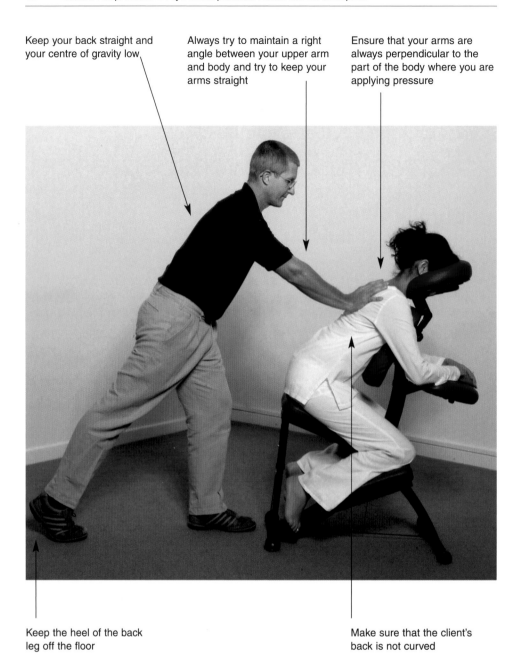

Keep the heel of the back leg off the floor

Make sure that the client's back is not curved

Figure 6.1: Posture is very important in the seated acupressure bodywork kata.

Point Location for the Left Shoulder and Upper Back

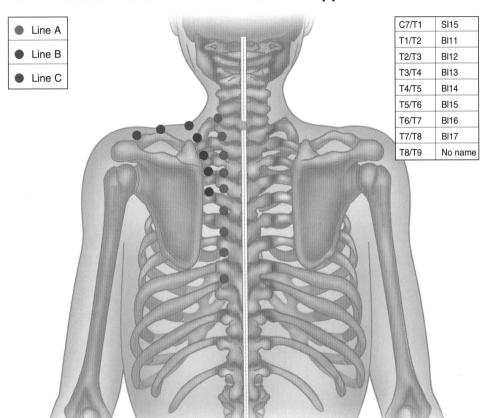

- ● Line A
- ● Line B
- ● Line C

C7/T1	SI15
T1/T2	Bl11
T2/T3	Bl12
T3/T4	Bl13
T4/T5	Bl14
T5/T6	Bl15
T6/T7	Bl16
T7/T8	Bl17
T8/T9	No name

Line A:

This follows the inner Bladder channel except for the 1st point. The Bladder channel runs down either side of the spine along the highest point of the erector spinae muscles. These points are 1.5 cun lateral to the centre line of the spine.

Point 1: Small Intestine 15. 2 cun lateral to C7/T1.

Point 2: Bladder 11. Between T1/T2.

Point 3: Bladder 12. Between T2/T3.

Point 4: Bladder 13. Between T3/T4.

Point 5: Bladder 14. Between T4/T5.

Point 6: Bladder 15. Between T5/T6.

Point 7: Bladder 16. Between T6/T7.

Point 8: Bladder 17. Between T7/T8.

Point 9: No name.   Between T8/T9.

Line B:

This follows the outer Bladder channel, and runs 3 cun lateral to the centre line or down the medial border of the scapula, on roughly the lateral edge of the erector spinae muscles.

Point 1: Small Intestine 14. Medial and superior to the medial border of the scapula level with C7/T1 and approximately 3 cun lateral to the centre line.

Point 2: Bladder 41. Between T1/T2.

Point 3: Bladder 42. Between T2/T3.

Point 4: Bladder 43. Between T3/T4.

Line C:

Point 1: No name. On the top of the shoulder at the angle where the neck joins the shoulder.

Point 2: Gallbladder 21. On top of the shoulder midway between C7 and the lateral edge of the acromion process. This point is roughly on the nipple line.

Point 3: Large Intestine 16. On top of the shoulder in the hollow which is formed in the angle where the clavicle meets the spine of the scapula.

The Left Shoulder and Upper Back Routine

Repeat all moves twice.

Opening Contact

Make two-handed contact with your client's upper back and shoulder area and briefly tune in. Brush across the shoulders and rub briskly for a few seconds.

Double Palm Press

Place your hands on the middle of the back at about the level of T5 with your arms straight, wrists together and fingers pointing outwards. Palm down the middle of the erector spinae muscles in five equally spaced positions, finishing just above the level of the iliac crest.

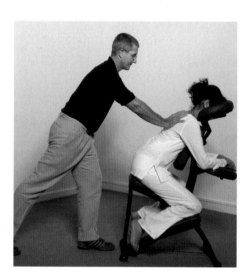

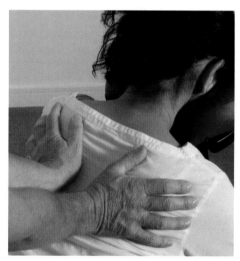

When working on these points, it is important not to work too deeply on weak or frail clients. Use your thumbs instead. Gallbladder 21 is contraindicated in pregnancy.

Kneading

Brush across the shoulders and upper back, and rub briskly to warm the area and stimulate the nerve response. Using your palms, thumbs and fingers, knead the shoulders and then down either side of the spinal column, getting a sense of the underlying anatomy, areas of specific tension, or abnormalities. Work freestyle, introducing your touch to the client and warming the underlying muscles. Work from the base of the neck down to the sacral area, keeping the arms straight and shoulders, elbows and hands in a straight line and at a 90° angle to your body.

Stretching Away From the Spine

Stand slightly to the left side of the person in the chair with your left foot forward, right foot back and knead the erector spinae muscles on the opposite side of the body firmly with a slightly circular motion, moving away from the spine. Work slowly down to the bottom of the ribs. Slide your working hand back up to the top of the back and repeat. Then using both hands, with the heel of the hand in the hollow between the spine and the muscles, press the muscles away from the spine. Only work down as far as the end of the thoracic vertebrae and repeat. Maintaining contact, move around to their right side and repeat.

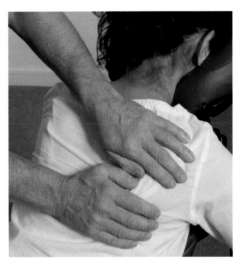

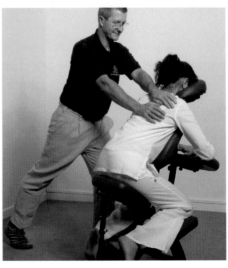

The Left Shoulder and Upper Back Routine

Archer's Arm

Step forward and to the left of your client with your left foot forward, right foot back and place the heel of your right hand over the muscle between the scapula and the spinous processes of the vertebral column, your fingers resting lightly over the spine itself. Keep your right elbow flexed. Drop your weight down through your arm to apply pressure in three evenly spaced positions, starting at the level of C7 and finishing level with the lower border of the scapula. Repeat.

Forearm Press

Stepping slightly further forward, place the fleshy underside of your forearm onto the top of the trapezius muscle and once again dropping your body weight, apply pressure to three positions on the muscle; starting by the neck and moving towards the shoulder.

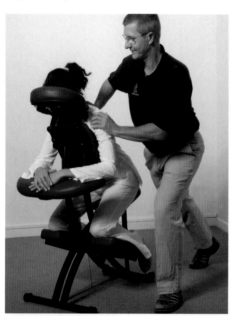

Elbow Press to Nine Points

Locate a point roughly two finger widths lateral to C7/T1, on the crest of the erector spinae muscles. They are halfway between the spinous process of the vertebrae and the medial border of the scapula. Then using the underside of your elbow, apply pressure to nine points down the back, starting opposite the gap between C7/T1 and finishing just below the inferior border of the scapula T8/T9. This starts with the Small Intestine channel and runs down the Bladder channel. Avoid pressing directly onto bone. Shuffle backwards as you move down the spine to maintain the correct angle of contact with the back and make sure you are not too far away from the spine as this may cause discomfort if you press on the ribs. Repeat.

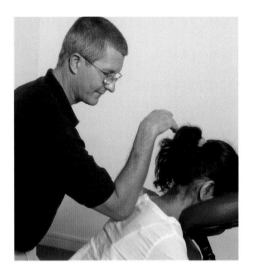

Note: It is quite difficult to judge the amount and quality of pressure you are giving with your elbows, so it is important to get feedback from your client when using this technique. Keep your wrists loose and your elbow at a right angle to the back, lean your body weight into your front leg to apply the pressure. If you find you cannot easily regulate the pressure, you can stand behind your client and apply pressure with your thumbs.

The Left Shoulder and Upper Back Routine

Forearm Rolling

Using the soft fleshy underside of your forearm, apply pressure down the medial border of the scapula, rolling your forearm slightly as you progress down. Work in this way in the area between T1 and T7.

Elbow Press

Step forward again and place the flat underside of your upper arm (just above your elbow) on the trapezius next to the neck. Then press three equally spaced points, working laterally towards the shoulder, finishing at the hollow where the clavicle meets the spine of the scapula.

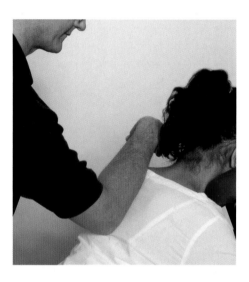

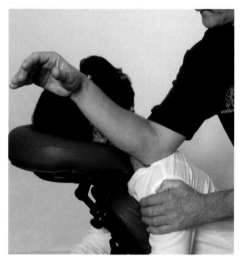

Point Location for the Outer Aspect of the Left Arm and Hand

Lines A, B and C	Line D	Line E	Line F	Hand

Lines A and B: Small Intestine and Triple Heater Meridians

There are no specific pressure points used here. The meridians are simply squeezed between the thumb and index finger of the right hand (Dragon's mouth). Work this way in 5 equally spaced places between the axilla and the elbow.

Line C: Large Intestine Meridian

5 equally spaced points from the shoulder to the elbow.

Point 1: Large Intestine 15. In the front dimple at the shoulder when the arm is raised slightly.

Point 2: No name. Found midway between points 1 and 3.

Point 3: Large Intestine 14. At the lowest end (insertion) of the deltoideus muscle, midway between points 1 and 5.

Point 4: No name. Midway between points 3 and 5.

Point 5: Large Intestine 12. 1 cun above the elbow crease, superior to the lateral epicondyle when the elbow is held at a right angle.

Line D: Large Intestine Meridian

Point 1: Large Intestine 11. On the lateral end of the elbow crease.

Point 2: Large Intestine 10. 2 cun or 3 finger widths below LI11.

Point 3: No name. Midway between LI11 (point 1) and LI5 (point 5).

Point 4: No name. Midway between point 3 and LI5 (point 5).

Point 5: Large Intestine 5. In the anatomical snuffbox, at the radial side of the wrist between the two tendons highlighted when the thumb is abducted.

Line E: Small Intestine Meridian

With the ulna facing away from the body (palm to the rear), line E is found in the groove between the flexor muscles and the ulna.

Point 1: No name. In a hollow just below the olecranon process.

Point 2: No name. Midway between points 1 and 3.

Point 3: Small Intestine 7. Midway between points 1 and 5.

Point 4: No name. Midway between points 3 and 5.

Point 5: Small Intestine 5. In the gap between the head of the ulna and the carpals (triquetral bone).

Line F: Triple Heater Meridian

This meridian follows a line along the posterior surface of the arm from the elbow to the wrist crease and is above the gap between the radius and ulna.

Point 1: No name. A thumb's width below the elbow on a line with the middle finger.

Point 2: No name. Midway between points 1 and 3.

Point 3: Triple Heater 9. Midway between the elbow and the wrist, in a groove which can be felt between the extensor muscles.

Point 4: No name. Midway between points 3 and 5.

Point 5: Triple Heater 4. On the ulnar side of the tendon that can be found in the middle of the wrist crease.

Hand Point: Large Intestine 4

This point is found on the dorsal surface of the hand in the web between the thumb and index finger. If the client lightly presses these two fingers together, LI4 can be located at the end of the crease approximately in the highest point of the muscle, and is stimulated by applying pressure towards the first metacarpal and angled slightly below it.

The Outer Aspect of the Left Arm and Hand Routine

Repeat all moves twice.

Arm Shake

Squat or kneel to the left side of your client. Take their arm between your hands and shake or roll the arm, moving briskly down from the shoulder to the wrist. This will help to loosen any tension in the shoulders.

Thumb Squeeze

Line A

Drop their arm down by their side and squat down facing them. With your right hand acting as a mother hand, support their elbow and squeeze their triceps brachii muscle between your thumb and forefingers, rolling it slightly towards you. Work five equally spaced positions from the deltoideus muscle to the elbow.

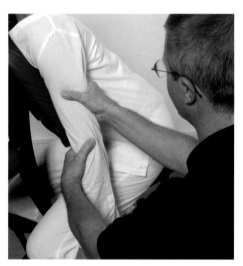

Line B

With your left hand acting as a mother hand, support their elbow and squeeze their biceps brachii muscle between your thumb and forefingers, rolling it slightly towards you. Again, work five equally spaced positions down the upper arm.

Thumb Press

Line C

Bring both hands up to the level of the axilla and grip the biceps brachii and triceps brachii muscles by placing the thumbs together on the side of the arm. Squeeze five points in this way, working down from the deltoideus muscle to the elbow.

Line D

Turn their hand so that it faces forward and work five points down the radius, starting at the elbow crease and finishing at the anatomical snuffbox.

Line E

Turn their hand to face the rear and change the mother hand. Work five points down the crest of the ulna starting at the elbow crease and finishing just below the styloid process of the ulna.

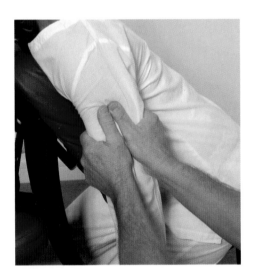

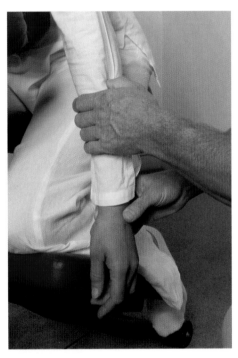

Line F

Bring your right hand down to their wrist and support the arm. Using your left hand, squeeze their forearm between your thumb and forefingers, pressing five equally spaced points between the elbow and wrist, starting in the hollow just below the elbow and ending in the middle of the wrist crease.

The Outer Aspect of the Left Arm and Hand Routine

Wrist Flex and Squeeze

Supporting above their wrist with both hands, flick the wrist back and forth to release any tension. Using your left hand to support their wrist, take hold of their fingers and rotate gently in both directions. Then flex and extend the wrist to gently stretch the tendons. Squeeze the sides of the wrist between your thumb and index finger.

Shoulder Rotations

Step back behind them and scooping your left arm under their elbow, support their left shoulder with your left hand. Place your right hand over their left scapula and circle their shoulder, rotating their arm in a backwards direction. Repeat several times. Then, supporting the scapula, securely move the whole shoulder girdle and the scapula over the ribs.

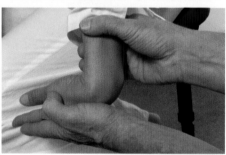

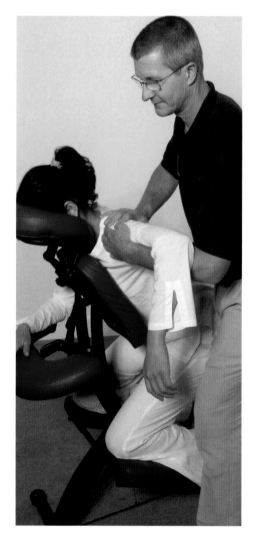

Chicken Wing – Thumbs Under Scapula

Lower their arm and bring it behind their back into the chicken wing position. Draw their scapula back onto your right thumb or four fingers. Repeat several times, moving up and down the length of the medial border of the scapula.

Arm Stretch

Bring their arm around to the front of their body. Step forward far enough to allow you to stretch their arm forward whilst supporting under their elbow with your right hand, and at their wrist with your left.

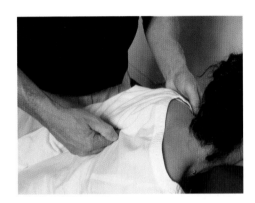

The Outer Aspect of the Left Arm and Hand Routine

Hand Spread, Thumb Strokes and Jiggles

Place their arm back on the armrest and squeeze the sides of the wrist. Spread open the back of the hand using the heels of your hand. Then, with the pads of your thumbs, stroke down between and the outer metacarpals of the hand. Then 'jiggle' your thumbs between the outer metacarpals. Repeat this with the inner metacarpals.

Finish with the outside of the arm by locating LI4 and squeezing for two seconds.

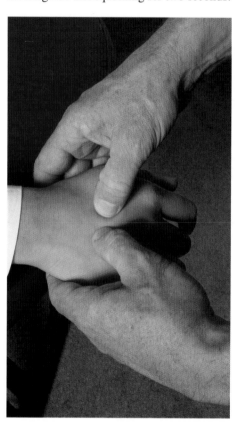
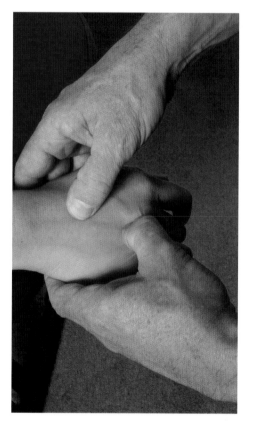

Point Location for the Inner Aspect of the Left Arm and Hand

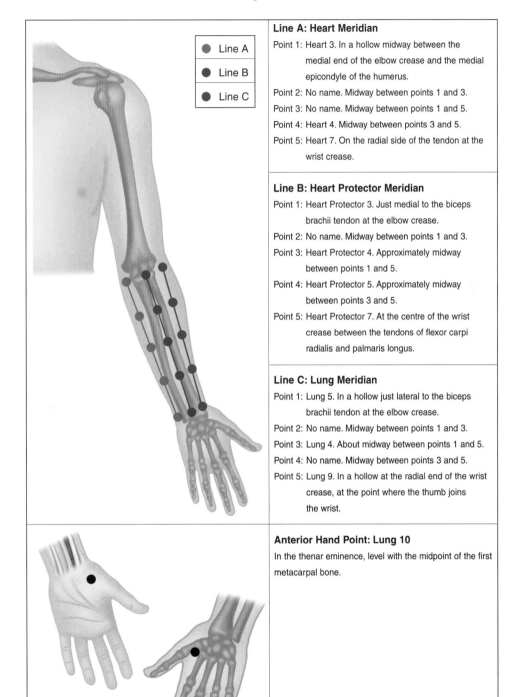

- ● Line A
- ● Line B
- ● Line C

Line A: Heart Meridian

Point 1: Heart 3. In a hollow midway between the medial end of the elbow crease and the medial epicondyle of the humerus.

Point 2: No name. Midway between points 1 and 3.

Point 3: No name. Midway between points 1 and 5.

Point 4: Heart 4. Midway between points 3 and 5.

Point 5: Heart 7. On the radial side of the tendon at the wrist crease.

Line B: Heart Protector Meridian

Point 1: Heart Protector 3. Just medial to the biceps brachii tendon at the elbow crease.

Point 2: No name. Midway between points 1 and 3.

Point 3: Heart Protector 4. Approximately midway between points 1 and 5.

Point 4: Heart Protector 5. Approximately midway between points 3 and 5.

Point 5: Heart Protector 7. At the centre of the wrist crease between the tendons of flexor carpi radialis and palmaris longus.

Line C: Lung Meridian

Point 1: Lung 5. In a hollow just lateral to the biceps brachii tendon at the elbow crease.

Point 2: No name. Midway between points 1 and 3.

Point 3: Lung 4. About midway between points 1 and 5.

Point 4: No name. Midway between points 3 and 5.

Point 5: Lung 9. In a hollow at the radial end of the wrist crease, at the point where the thumb joins the wrist.

Anterior Hand Point: Lung 10

In the thenar eminence, level with the midpoint of the first metacarpal bone.

The Inner Aspect of the Left Arm and Hand Routine

Thumb Press

Line A

Turn over (supinate) your client's arm, adjusting the elbow position for comfort if necessary and support it with your right mother hand. Using your left thumb, press into five equally spaced points in a line from the medial side of the elbow crease, finishing on the ulnar side of the wrist crease. Repeat.

Palm Spread and Stretch

Spread open the palm of your client's hand using the heels of your hands, and linking your little fingers between their thumb and index finger, and ring and little fingers. Stretch out their palm and work the thenar and hypothenar eminences with your thumbs.

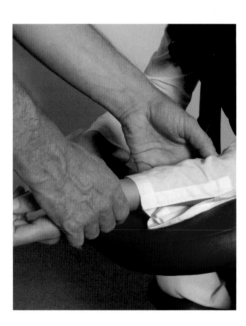
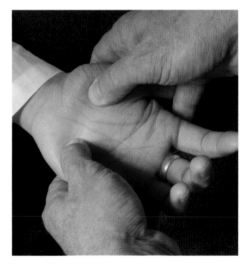

Line B

Repeat the above process twice down a line from the midline of the elbow crease, just medial to the biceps brachii tendon, to a point on the middle of the wrist crease.

Line C

Repeat the above process twice along a line running from a hollow at the end of the elbow crease to a point on the wrist at the base of the thumb.

Thumb Strokes and Jiggles

Using the pads of your thumbs, stroke down between the outer metacarpals of the hand. Then 'jiggle' your thumbs down the same line. Repeat this with the inner metacarpals. Locate Lung 10 and squeeze for two seconds.

Coin Rubs

Rub briskly down from the base of the thumb to the tip of the thumb, as if polishing a coin between your fingers and thumb, pulling towards you slightly. Repeat this action down the sides of the thumb.

Nail Point Squeeze

Squeeze the nail points between your thumb and forefinger for a second.

Fingertip Snap

Bring your index finger onto the nail and squeeze the finger between the second and third fingers. Pull off briskly with a snap. Work all the fingers from the thumb to the little finger.

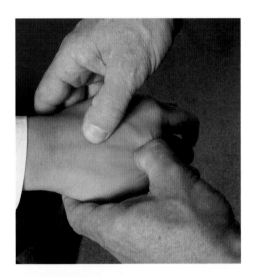

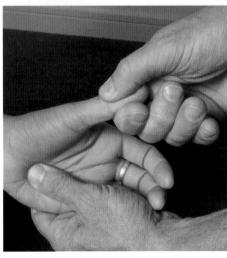
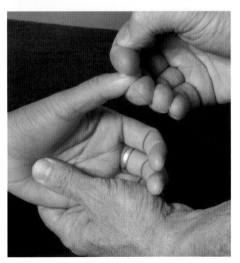

The Inner Aspect of the Left Arm and Hand Routine

Arm Stretch

Turn over (pronate) your partner's arm and grasp the wrist with your thumbs just behind the wrist crease. Lift your client's arm, bringing it in line with their body. Ask them to breathe in. As they exhale, give a gentle stretch along their arm and into their shoulder. Place the arm back onto the armrest.

Shoulder Kneading

Bring your hands up onto the client's shoulders and knead both shoulders for a few seconds. Then brush lightly across the shoulders in a lateral direction.

Maintaining contact, walk around to their right side and position yourself ready for the single palm or Archer's arm press.

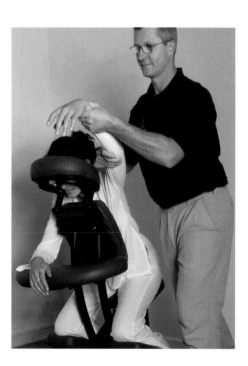

Point Location for the Right Shoulder and Upper Back

C7/T1	SI15
T1/T2	BI11
T2/T3	BI12
T3/T4	BI13
T4/T5	BI14
T5/T6	BI15
T6/T7	BI16
T7/T8	BI17
T8/T9	No name

- ● Line A
- ● Line B
- ● Line C

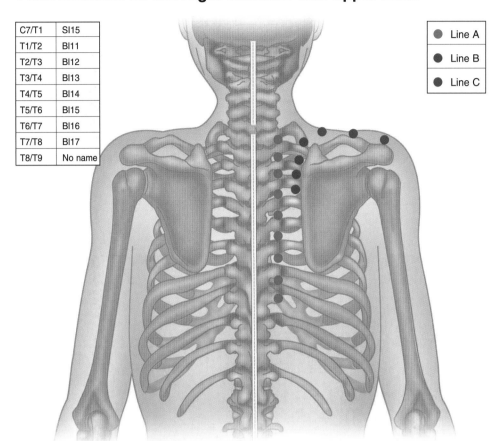

Line A:

This follows the inner Bladder channel except for the 1st point. The Bladder channel runs down either side of the spine along the highest point of the erector spinae muscles. These points are 1.5 cun lateral to the centre line of the spine.

Point 1: Small Intestine 15. 2 cun lateral to C7/T1.

Point 2: Bladder 11. Between T1/T2.

Point 3: Bladder 12. Between T2/T3.

Point 4: Bladder 13. Between T3/T4.

Point 5: Bladder 14. Between T4/T5.

Point 6: Bladder 15. Between T5/T6.

Point 7: Bladder 16. Between T6/T7.

Point 8: Bladder 17. Between T7/T8.

Point 9: No name.   Between T8/T9.

Line B:

This follows the outer Bladder channel and runs 3 cun lateral to the centre line or down the medial border of the scapula, on roughly the lateral edge of the erector spinae muscles.

Point 1: Small Intestine 14. Medial and superior to the medial border of the scapula level with C7/T1 and approximately 3 cun lateral to the centre line.

Point 2: Bladder 41. Between T1/T2.

Point 3: Bladder 42. Between T2/T3.

Point 4: Bladder 43. Between T3/T4.

Line C

Point 1: No name. On the top of the shoulder, at the angle where the neck joins the shoulder.

Point 2: Gallbladder 21. On top of the shoulder midway between C7 and the lateral edge of the acromion process. This point is roughly on the nipple line.

Point 3: Large Intestine 16. On top of the shoulder, in the hollow which is formed in the angle where the clavicle meets the spine of the scapula.

The Right Shoulder and Upper Back Routine

Repeat all moves twice.

Archer's Arm

Step forward and to the right of your client with your right foot forward, left foot back. Place the heel of your right hand over the muscle between the scapula and the spinous processes of the vertebral column, with your fingers resting lightly over the spine itself. Keep your left elbow flexed. Drop your weight down through your arm to apply pressure in three evenly spaced

Forearm Press

Stepping slightly further forward, place the fleshy underside of your forearm onto the top of the trapezius muscle. Then, by dropping your body weight, apply pressure to three positions on the muscle, starting by the neck and moving towards the shoulder.

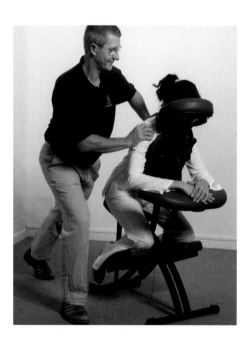

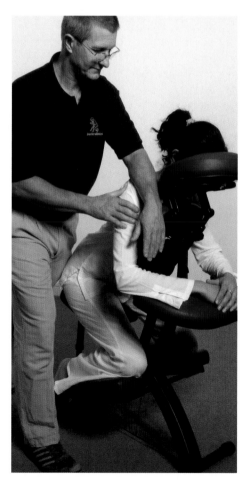

positions, starting at the level of C7 and finishing level with the lower border of the scapula.

When working on these points, it is important not to work too deeply on weak or frail clients. Use your thumbs instead. Gallbladder 21 is contraindicated in pregnancy.

Elbow Press to Nine Points

Locate a point roughly two finger widths lateral to C7/T1, on the crest of the erector spinae muscles. The points you are about to stimulate are halfway between the spinous process of the vertebrae and the medial border of the scapula. Using the underside of your elbow, apply pressure to nine points down the back, starting opposite the gap between C7/T1 and finishing just below the inferior border of the scapula T8/T9. This sequence starts with the Small Intestine channel and runs down the Bladder channel. Be careful you are not pressing on bone.

Note: It is quite difficult to judge the amount and quality of pressure you are giving with your elbows, so it is important to get feedback from your client when using this technique. If you find you cannot easily regulate the pressure, you can stand behind your client and apply pressure with your thumbs.

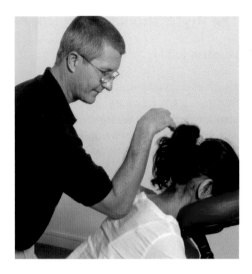

The Right Shoulder and Upper Back Routine

Forearm Rolling

Using the soft fleshy underside of your forearm, apply pressure down along the medial border of the scapula. Roll your forearm slightly as you progress down. Work in this way in the area between T1 and T7.

Elbow Press

Step forward again and place the flat underside of your upper arm just above the elbow on the trapezius next to the neck. Press three equally spaced points: working laterally towards the shoulder. Finish at the hollow where the clavicle meets the spine of the scapula.

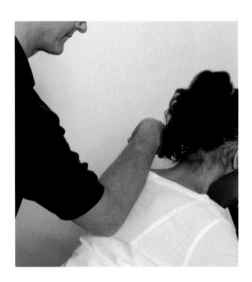

Point Location for the Outer Aspect of the Right Arm and Hand

Lines A, B and C	Line D	Line E	Line F	Hand

Lines A and B: Small Intestine and Triple Heater Meridians

There are no specific pressure points used here. The meridians are simply squeezed between the thumb and index finger of the right hand (Dragon's mouth). Work this way in 5 equally spaced places between the axilla and the elbow.

Line C: Large Intestine Meridian

Five equally spaced points from the shoulder to the elbow.

Point 1: Large Intestine 15. In the front dimple at the shoulder when the arm is raised slightly.

Point 2: No name. Found midway between points 1 and 3.

Point 3: Large Intestine 14. At the lowest end (insertion) of the deltoideus muscle, midway between points 1and 5.

Point 4: No name. Midway between points 3 and 5.

Point 5: Large Intestine 12. 1 cun above the elbow crease, superior to the lateral epicondyle when the elbow is held at a right angle.

Line D: Large Intestine Meridian

Point 1: Large Intestine 11. On the lateral end of the elbow crease.

Point 2: Large Intestine 10. 2 cun or 3 finger widths below LI11.

Point 3: No name. Midway between LI11 (point 1) and LI5 (point 5).

Point 4: No name. Midway between point 3 and LI5 (point 5).

Point 5: Large Intestine 5. In the anatomical snuffbox, located at the radial side of the wrist between the two tendons highlighted when the thumb is abducted.

Line E: Small Intestine Meridian

With the ulna facing away from the body (palm to the rear), this is found in the groove between the flexor muscles and the ulna.

Point 1: No name. This is located in a hollow just below the olecranon process.

Point 2: No name. Midway between points 1 and 3.

Point 3: Small Intestine 7. Midway between points 1 and 5.

Point 4: No name. Midway between points 3 and 5.

Point 5: Small Intestine 5. In the gap between the head of the ulna and the carpals (triquetral bone).

Line F: Triple Heater Meridian

This meridian follows a line along the posterior surface of the arm from the elbow to the wrist crease, and is above the gap between the radius and ulna.

Point 1: No name. About a thumb's width below the elbow on a line with the middle finger.

Point 2: No name. Midway between points 1 and 3.

Point 3: Triple Heater 9. Midway between the elbow and the wrist, in a groove which can be felt between the extensor muscles.

Point 4: No name. Midway between points 3 and 5.

Point 5: Triple Heater 4. On the ulnar side of the tendon that can be found in the middle of the wrist crease.

Hand Point: Large Intestine 4

This point is found on the dorsal surface of the hand in the web between the thumb and index finger. If the client lightly presses these two fingers together, LI4 can be located at the end of the crease approximately in the highest point of the muscle, and is stimulated by applying pressure towards the first metacarpal and angled slightly below it.

The Outer Aspect of the Right Arm and Hand Routine

Hand Spread, Thumb Strokes and Jiggles

Place their arm back on the armrest and squeeze the sides of the wrist. Spread open the back of the hand using the heels of your hand. Then, with the pads of your thumbs stroke down between the outer metacarpals of the hand. Then 'jiggle' your thumbs between the outer metacarpals. Repeat this with the inner metacarpals.

Finish with the outside of the arm by locating LI4 and squeezing for two seconds.

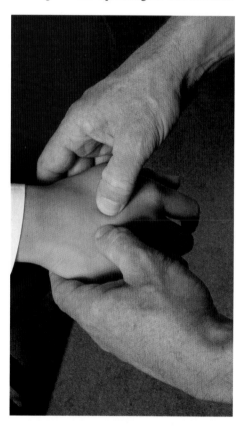
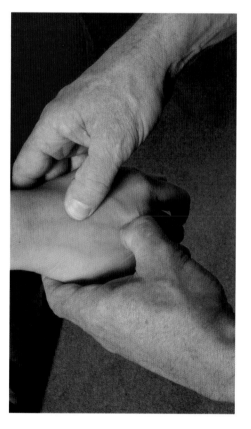

Point Location for the Inner Aspect of the Right Arm and Hand

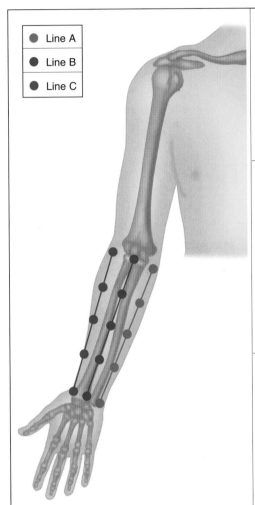

- ● Line A
- ● Line B
- ● Line C

Line A: Heart Meridian

Point 1: Heart 3. In a hollow midway between the medial end of the elbow crease and the medial epicondyle of the humerus.

Point 2: No name. Midway between points 1 and 3.

Point 3: No name. Midway between points 1 and 5.

Point 4: Heart 4. Midway between points 3 and 5.

Point 5: Heart 7. On the radial side of the tendon at the wrist crease.

Line B: Heart Protector Meridian

Point 1: Heart Protector 3. Just medial to the biceps brachii tendon at the elbow crease.

Point 2: No name. Midway between points 1 and 3.

Point 3: Heart Protector 4. Approximately midway between points 1 and 5.

Point 4: Heart Protector 5. Approximately midway between points 3 and 5.

Point 5: Heart Protector 7. At the centre of the wrist crease between the tendons of flexor carpi radialis and palmaris longus.

Line C: Lung Meridian

Point 1: Lung 5. In a hollow just lateral to the biceps brachii tendon at the elbow crease.

Point 2: No name. Midway between points 1 and 3.

Point 3: Lung 4. About midway between points 1 and 5.

Point 4: No name. Midway between points 3 and 5.

Point 5: Lung 9. In a hollow at the radial end of the wrist crease, at the point where the thumb joins the wrist.

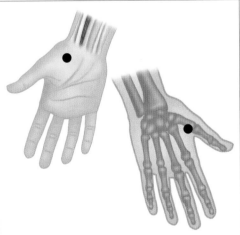

Anterior Hand Point: Lung 10

On the thenar eminence, level with the midpoint of the first metacarpal bone.

The Inner Aspect of the Right Arm and Hand Routine

Thumb Press

Line A

Turn over (supinate) your client's arm, adjusting their elbow position for comfort if necessary, and support it with your right mother hand. Using your left thumb, press into five equally spaced points in a line from the medial side of the elbow crease, finishing on the ulnar side of the wrist crease. Repeat.

Palm Spread and Stretch

Spread open the palm of your client's hand using the heels of your hands, and linking your little fingers between their thumb and index finger, and ring and little fingers. Stretch out their palm and work the thenar and hypothenar eminences with your thumbs.

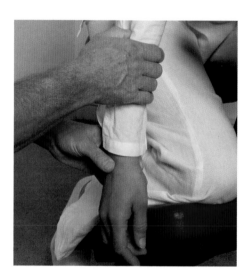 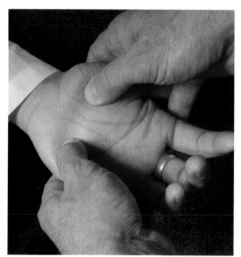

Line B

Repeat the above process twice down a line from the midline of the elbow crease, just medial to the biceps brachii tendon, to a point on the middle of the wrist crease.

Line C

Repeat the above process twice along a line running from a hollow at the end of the elbow crease to a point on the wrist at the base of the thumb.

Thumb Strokes and Jiggles

Using the pads of your thumbs, stroke down between the outer metacarpals of the hand. Then 'jiggle' your thumbs down the same line. Repeat this with the inner metacarpals. Locate Lung 10 and squeeze for two seconds.

Coin Rubs

Rub briskly down from the base of the thumb to the tip, as if polishing a coin between your fingers and thumb, pulling towards you slightly. Repeat this action down the sides of the thumb.

Nail Point Squeeze

Squeeze the nail points between your thumb and forefinger for a second.

Fingertip Snap

Bring your index finger onto the nail and squeeze their finger between your second and third fingers. Pull off briskly with a snap. Work all their fingers from the thumb to the little finger.

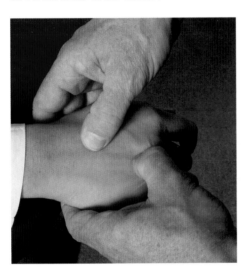

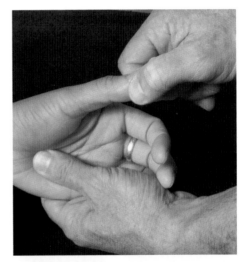

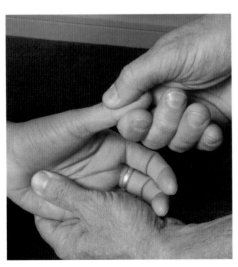

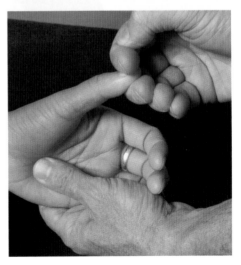

The Lower Back and Sacrum Routine

Warming Low Back

Stand slightly to one side of the person in the chair and briskly rub the erector spinae muscles of the lower back, from the end of the ribcage to the sacrum.

Double Palm Press

Move into the basic stance, facing the receiver's back. Double palm press five equally spaced points, starting from a position just below the inferior angle of the scapula and working down to the iliac crest. Repeat. Ensure your shoulders, elbows and hands are all in a straight line and at a right angle to your body.

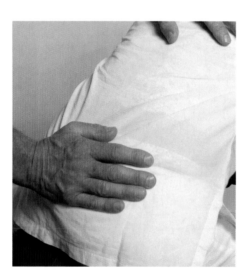 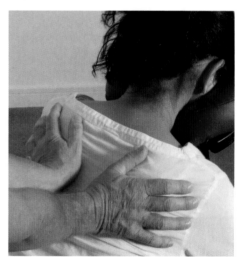

Single Palm Press

Move slightly forward with your left foot in front and your right leg directly behind your working hand. Place the heel of your right hand over the erector spinae muscle on the left of the spine, with your fingers cupping lightly over the spinal column. Your left hand rests lightly on their left shoulder. Press down five equally spaced points, beginning at about the level of T8/T9 and finish just superior to the iliac crest.

Thumb Press

Stand directly behind your client. Supporting your right thumb in between your left thumb and index finger, press down onto nine evenly spaced points along the erector spinae muscle to the left of the spine (Line A). Start at the level of T8/T9 and finish at L4/L5. Repeat. Make sure you keep your arms straight and that you are directly behind the area you are working on. Keep the flat of your left hand in contact with their back for support. Repeat the above two movements on the right side of the spine.

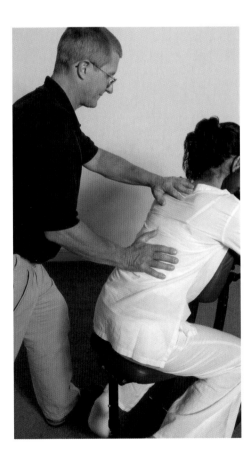

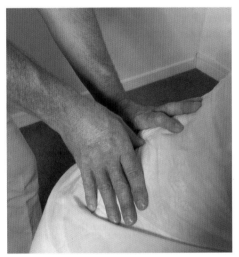

Sacral Points

Work the points on both sides of the sacrum (Line B) in a similar way.

The Neck and Head Routine

Occipital Release

Slide your fingers up under the occiput and stretch lightly backwards, using your fingertips to work in small circles along the occipital ridge; moving laterally from the central line out towards the mastoid process (Line A bilaterally).

Spider Press-ups

Using your fingertips, work up into their scalp as if washing their hair. Imagine your fingers are spiders doing press-ups.

Crab Grabs

Use the pads of your fingers to grip the scalp and pull away quickly (crab grabs). Repeat this several times.

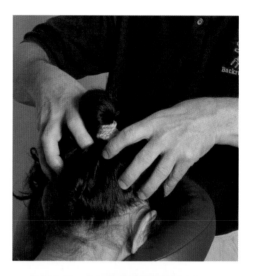

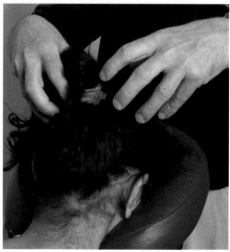

Thumbs Along Bladder Channel

Finally, work the Bladder channel backwards, one thumb's width away from the centre line of the cranium, for as much of its length as you can.

Brush Down

Bring both hands onto their shoulders and brush off twice.

Double Palm Press

Maintaining two-handed contact, move around to face their back and double palm press twice on five equally spaced points down the back.

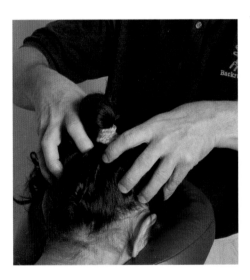

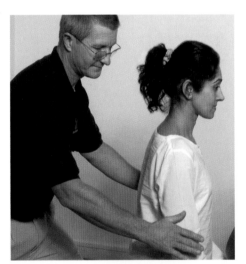

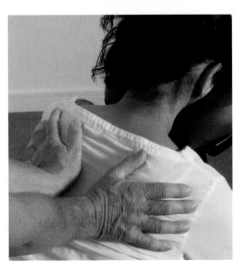

Percussion Techniques

Hacking

Using the sides of your hands, 'karate chop' style, hack across the back from the centre line to the edge of the trapezius muscle and back. Then hack in a line down the erector spinae muscle to the lower end of the ribcage and back again. Repeat twice on each side of the spine. This will form a T shaped pattern.

Prayer Hands

Pressing the palms of your hands together (prayer hands), repeat the above movement twice. This gives slightly more weight to the technique.

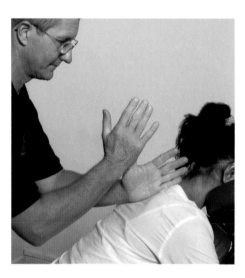

**Curled Fist or Cupped
Hands Percussion**

Form loose fists or cupped hands and repeat
the above movement twice. When using the
cupped hands, they should be lightly clasped
palm to palm, and on connecting with the
back should make a squishing noise. The
emphasis should be on lifting off the body
rather than on the downward stroke.

Cross Stitch Percussion

When performing prayer hands and cupped
hands percussion, finish the technique by
working up and down either side of the
spine in a 'cross stitch pattern', tapping
alternately on each side of the thoracic
vertebrae.

Brush Down

Brush down twice from the top of the back
to the sacrum, allowing your hands to flow
in one smooth movement.

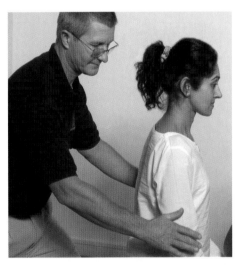

The Finishing Stretch!

Sit Upright

Step to one side and place one hand on their lower back and the other on the crown of their head. Ask them to very slowly sit up with their arms hanging by their sides.

Double Forearm Press

Move back behind them and place your forearms on their shoulders and gently press down. Be very careful not to press too hard and exaggerate their natural lumbar curve and compress the vertebrae.

Neck Stretch

Leaving your left arm in place, place your right arm over their head so your fingers are by their left ear. Gently draw their head over to the right as far as it will naturally go (explain to them what you are going to do). Ask them to take a deep breath in. As they breathe out, gently stretch down on their left shoulder. Repeat to the other side.

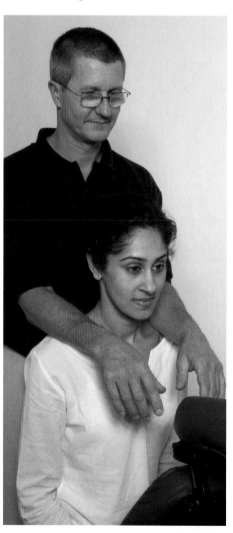

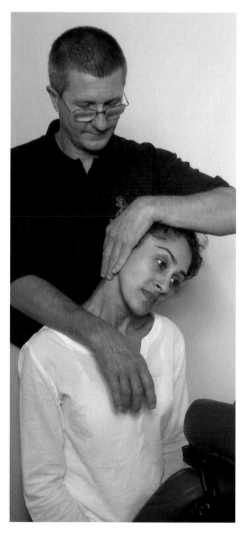

Penguin Stretch

Reach under their elbows from the back and take hold of their forearms. Ask them to inhale. As they exhale, stretch backwards and upwards. Again, explain to the client what you are doing as you perform this stretch.

Angel Stretch

Bring their arms up in a circular movement until they can clasp their hands behind their head. Reach up under their arms. Ask them to inhale, and as they exhale, stretch their arms backwards. Clasp their wrists and using a circular motion, bring their arms back down by their sides. Knead their shoulders for a few seconds.

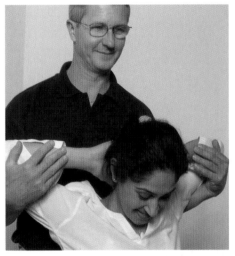

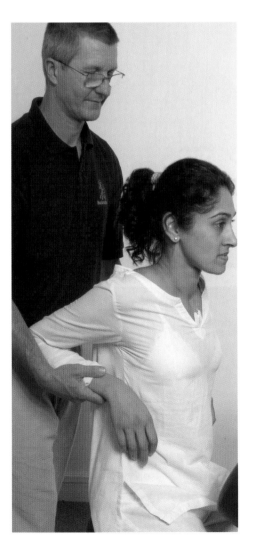

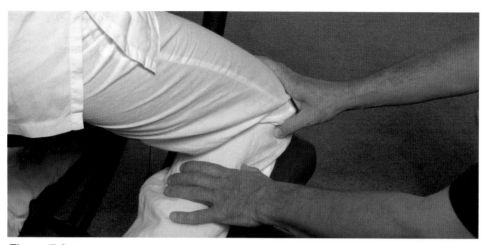

Figure 7.3.

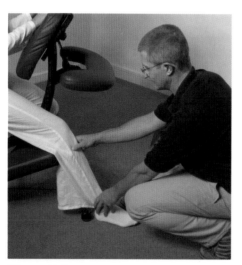 

Figure 7.4.

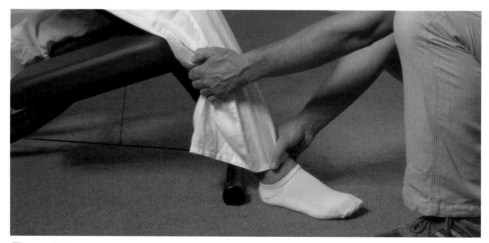

Figure 7.5.

With your client's leg still on the shin supports, locate the head of the fibula with your left hand and divide the distance between this point and a point just anterior and inferior to the lateral malleolus (ankle bone) into five. This is the Gallbladder meridian. Using your thumb, gently work down the leg from knee to ankle twice (*see* figure 7.3).

Place your client's foot on the floor and move around to face their leg. The Stomach channel continues on a line from the lateral border of the patella to the centre of the ankle joint. Support their knee with your left hand and work the channel with the thumb of your right, again dividing the leg into five equal points (*see* figure 7.4).

Support the knee with your right hand and work five equally spaced points down the medial side of the leg, along the crest of the tibia from just below the knee to a point anterior and inferior to the medial malleolus. This is the Spleen channel.

Still supporting the knee with your left hand, reach behind their lower leg with your right hand and lean back, drawing their gastrocnemius muscle towards you; wrapping it around the bone. Repeat this several times, working down the leg before changing support hand and pulling the muscle the other way. This is called a 'cross-fibre' technique and is wonderful for releasing tension in the legs (*see* figure 7.5). Replace your client's leg onto the shin rest and then repeat on their left leg. It is important to remember not to work the lower legs of a pregnant woman.

Some Common Mistakes

It is possible that you may make some common errors when you first start to practice seated acupressure bodywork, and similar mistakes and bad habits may creep in over time. Some of the most common errors are listed below:

- Chair – Incorrect height or angle;
- Basic posture – Swinging hips forward;
- Erector spinae muscles – Kneading and stretching away below the ribs;
- Archer's arm – Body position too far back. Leaning in towards the body, not maintaining 90° angle;
- Forearm press – Body not far enough forward. Incorrect angle of pressure;
- Elbow press – Wrist not relaxed. Working (back) foot not behind working hand. Not 'squiggling' back to keep correct body angle;
- Elbow onto shoulder – Incorrect point of contact on elbow. Incorrect angle of pressure. Body too far back;
- Biceps / triceps brachii – Pinching;
- General arm work – Holding the arm too far from the body;
- Thumb press – Incorrect angle. Jabbing / prodding;
- Neck work – Jabbing / poking. Incorrect angle of pressure under the occiput. Pinching;
- Percussion techniques – Stiff wrists. No rhythm. Working below end of the ribcage;
- Forearm press – Pressing too hard and exaggerating the lumbar curve.

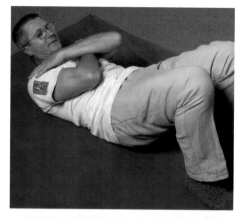

1a: The Pelvic Tilt

Lie on your back with your knees bent and cross your arms in front of your chest, placing each hand lightly on the opposite shoulder. Contract your abdominal muscles, drawing your stomach towards your spine. Tilt your pelvis and roll up your tailbone and sacrum. This will press and flatten your lower back onto the floor. Simultaneously tip your chin to your chest. Do not raise your buttocks off the floor. Hold this position for 30 seconds, maintaining the contraction in your abdominal muscles, and feeling your back pressed into the floor.

1b: Knee to Chest Tuck

Continuing from the pelvic tilt, pull your knees tightly into your chest and support them with your arms held just below the knees. As a result, you should feel the bones in your spine stretching apart. Gently rock your knees slightly closer into your chest and repeat the rocking motion 10–15 times. Repeat the pelvic tilt and knee to chest exercise at least 10 times.

2: Single Knee to Chest Stretch

Start from the basic pelvic tilt exercise with your back pressed firmly to the floor and the abdominal muscles held tight. Raise your head and shoulders off the floor. Bend your right knee and hold it at 45° to your chest. Extend your left leg and hold it 45° to the floor. Hold yourself in this position for 30 seconds and then slowly reverse the position of your legs. Repeat the sequence 10 times.

3a: The Angry Cat

Position yourself on your hands and knees, with your hands shoulder width apart, hands below your shoulders and knees below your hips. Do not allow your spine to sag downwards. Simultaneously contract your abdominal muscles and arch your back up towards the ceiling. Try to ensure as much of your lumbar spine is arched as possible. Hold this position for 30 seconds.

3b: The Child's Pose

From the stretched position above, sit back onto your heels and drop your body onto your knees. Stretch your arms out in front of you and feel the stretch pull your lumbar spine apart. Hold your head in a comfortable and relaxed position. Hold yourself in this position for 30 seconds. Repeat the angry cat and child's pose sequence at least 10 times, holding each position for 30 seconds.

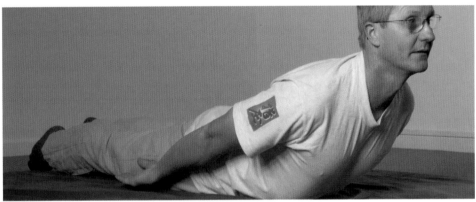

4: Multifidis Strengthening Exercise

Lie face down on a bed with your abdomen on the edge. Your navel should be on the edge of the bed. Have your arms by your side to provide extra support. Allow yourself to drop forwards and then raise your body up until you are parallel to the floor. Do not extend backwards. Hold this position for at least 30 seconds. Slowly lower yourself back down. If necessary ask someone to hold your legs. If you need extra weight on your upper body extend your arms forward past your head. Repeat the exercise 10 times.

5: Spinal Twists

Sit with your legs extended and shuffle back and forwards for a few seconds to relax into a comfortable position. Keep your left leg extended in front of you and bend the right leg to 45°. Place your right foot over the left leg and turn your upper body to the right, i.e. towards your bent knee. Using your left arm as a lever, slowly twist yourself. Make sure you turn your upper body and head as far as possible to the right and hold for 30 seconds. Release the stretch slowly and return to a central position before repeating to the other side. Repeat the exercise 10 times to each side.

Massage as we know it today can be traced to Per Henrik Ling (1776–1839). He was a Swedish gymnastics teacher and fencing master who tried to create a system of massage based on the movements he observed in Swedish gymnastics and other exercise systems. It was however a Dutch practitioner, Johan Georg Mezger (1838–1909), who developed it further and adopted the French names used to denote the basic strokes under which he systemized massage. Today Swedish massage is still generally defined by the original strokes that compose its method: *effleurage* (stroking), *petrissage* (kneading), *tapotement* (striking), *frictions* (rubbing), and *vibration*.

Many of these techniques were developed or copied from those that have been in use for thousands of years in the East, from Egypt to China. The earliest records of massage being used are found on scrolls found in a Chinese tomb dated around 1600 BC.

Many of the techniques used in the kata are similar if not identical to the techniques used in modern Swedish massage. Below is an explanation of the five basic strokes which make up the Swedish massage system.

Effleurage

Effleurage – the word means to 'stroke' – covers two distinct techniques in modern western massage: effleurage and stroking. In both techniques the hands move over the surface of the body in a similar fashion. In effleurage the hands are moved in the direction of the venous and lymphatic flow in order to promote the flow of blood and lymph through these vessels. When stroking, the hands move over the body in a much more random way, direction not being so important and the emphasis is placed on the sensory effect of the hands rather than moving blood or lymph. Effleurage and stroking are flowing, rhythmic movements which can vary in depth and pressure and cover the entire area being treated. When the movements are deep and slow they are relaxing whereas faster and more superficial movements have a tendency to be more uplifting and stimulating. When massaging the skin directly, effleurage techniques are used to apply the massage medium, oil, cream or talc and to connect other techniques. In seated acupressure bodywork, working through the clothes, no massage medium is used and clothes may sometimes prevent the strokes achieving their full potential – certain fabrics and designs can prove very difficult to work through. However these strokes can be used to warm up the body prior to using other stronger techniques or to fill in a gap if you find yourself wondering what to do next!

The equivalent techniques in Anma are Ma Fa – Rubbing and Mo Fa – Stroking.

Petrissage

Petrissage techniques include kneading, grasping, wringing and rolling. When applying petrissage the muscles and soft tissues are compressed against the underlying bony structure or squeezed and sometimes stretched and if performed correctly there will be a pumping effect on the blood and lymphatic vessels which will promote the flow and drainage of fluids in these vessels. They will also have a slight stretching effect on the muscles which will promote elasticity and mobility. These techniques are easily used in a seated acupressure massage routine and many of the techniques we have described in our kata are petrissage movements.

- Pressing the muscles away from the spine;
- Thumb squeeze to upper arm;
- Dragon's mouth to the neck;
- Cross fibre technique to the calf muscles.

The equivalent techniques in Anma are Rou Fa – Kneading, Na Fa – Grasping.

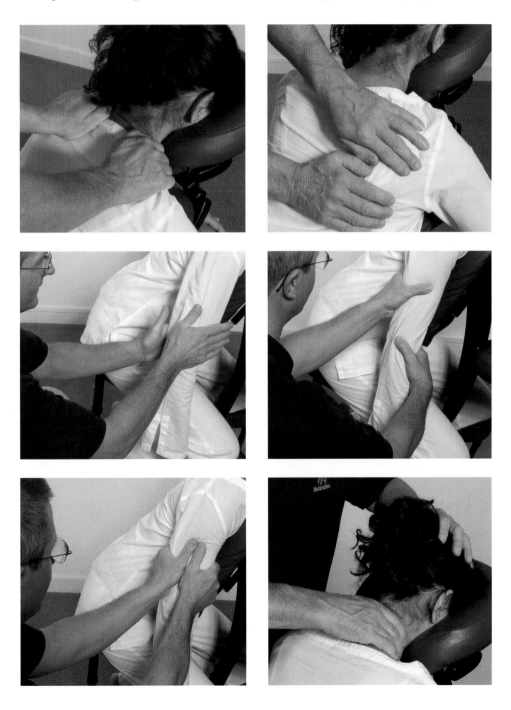

Tapotement

Tapotement or percussion are terms used to describe techniques where the body is repeatedly struck with the hands. Both hands are generally used and the movements must be rhythmic and flowing, with the hands or fingers striking alternately or together. Percussion techniques produce a reflex contraction which stimulates the muscles, increases the superficial circulation of the body, and softens hard adipose tissue under the skin. Typical percussion techniques are:

- Hacking;
- Chopping;

- Cupping or clapping;
- Beating.

These techniques are all very stimulating and are ideal for use in an on-site situation at the end of a chair massage to revitalise a client before they return to work. They can also be used with great success to soften very tight muscles very early on in the massage allowing you to work much deeper with acupressure techniques.

Karate chop hacking, prayer hands hacking and loose fist hacking used in our sequence are all examples of tapotement techniques.

The equivalent techniques in Anma are Ji Fa – Chopping, Pia Fa – Knocking.

Vibrations and Shaking

Vibrations and shaking are very differing techniques which involve producing a shaking or tremor in the soft tissue and muscles of the body. When applying a vibrating technique the working hand or fingers is placed on the part of the body to be worked on and vibrated up and down or side to side to produce a very fine tremor to a small area of the body. Vibrations are difficult to do well and need a lot of practice. This is ideally suited to acupressure massage as these fine and acurate movements can be used to disperse the energy from a specific acupressure point when there is an excess.

Shaking is not such a fine technique and can be applied to an individual muscle, a limb or to the entire body. When working a muscle it is usual to hold or grasp the muscle at its origin and insertion and loosely shake the area between your hands. If working a limb, grasp the hand or foot and shake the whole limb with a sideways or up and down motion. Shaking is an ideal technique for relaxing the muscles and can be very easily performed to the arms and back.

The equivalent techniques in Anma are Zhen Fa – Vibrations, Dou Fa – Shaking.

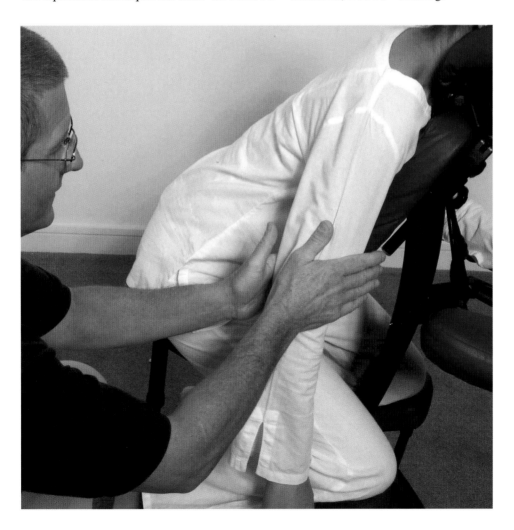

Friction and Frictions

Friction and frictions are again very different techniques, which sound very similar and are therefore often confused.

Friction is a fast, quite vigorous rubbing of the skin, which stimulates the local blood circulation and warms the area you are working on. Friction is a wonderful technique to use in a seated acupressure or on-site massage as it is so invigorating for tired achy muscles.

Friction is called Ca Fa in Anma massage.

Frictions in contrast are deep movements over a localized area where a firm pressure on the superficial tissues moves them over the tissue below. Frictions are commonly used to stimulate spinal nerves, to soften and stretch tight tissue and adhesions in muscles, to ease fibrositis or to massage ligaments and ease joint pain.

Frictions are a variation of the Anma technique called An Fa or pressing and can be easily introduced at any point of a seated acupressure massage treatment.

CHAPTER 10

Managing and Marketing Your Practice

Once you have successfully completed your training you may consider setting up yourself in business. As previously mentioned, the versatility of seated acupressure bodywork makes it an ideal full or part-time form of employment. The advantages of companies using seated acupressure bodywork in the workplace might include:

- Demands no capital investment by employers to instigate or maintain;
- It demonstrates the employers' commitment to the wellbeing of its employees;
- It revitalizes employees in twenty minutes leaving them refreshed and alert;
- Demands no effort or classes to attend, and nothing to learn or accomplish;
- Produces results in minutes, not days or weeks;
- Requires little or no motivation, as seated acupressure bodywork is enjoyable as well as therapeutic.

The advantages of seated acupressure bodywork in comparison to other forms of stress management might include:

- Other forms of stress management are generally provided after the period of stress has passed. Seated acupressure bodywork offers relief at the point when it is generally needed most, i.e. the stressful situation. And, it offers almost immediate results;
- Nearly all stress management systems require some sort of self-discipline or effort. Seated acupressure bodywork requires no effort from the client whatsoever; they simply have to sit back and let the practitioner do the work;
- Seated acupressure bodywork is popular with the majority of employees, usually resulting in a very high participation rate. This compares favourably with fitness classes and gymnasiums, which are used by relatively few;
- There are now recognized physical symptoms of stress, which include muscular tension, nerve sensitivity, aches and pains, anger and irritability and headaches. Seated acupressure bodywork works on these symptoms directly and immediately;
- Many other forms of stress management only offer information for the client to act upon. Whilst such information may be excellent in itself, it is only effective if acted upon. Seated acupressure bodywork only requires the client to turn up and sit in the massage chair whilst the practitioner does all the hard work;
- The value of any investment made by the company or the individual will be very quickly felt.

Where Can I Market Seated Acupressure Bodywork?

Due to its versatility, the lightness of the chair, and the fact that the client does not have to undress, seated acupressure bodywork can be used in a wide range of places and situations. Below are just a few examples, although the list is endless:

- In the office or workplace;
- In specialised shops, e.g. Walk-in Backrub;
- Health and fitness clubs;
- Airports; for both travellers and staff;
- Department stores and shopping centres;
- Nursing and convalescent homes;
- Hospitals;
- Mind, Body, Spirit shows and other public events;
- Hair and beauty salons;
- Sports events;
- Exhibitions and trade shows;
- Holiday camps;
- Golf and tennis clubs;
- Business clubs (Round Table, Rotary, Freemasons, etc.);
- Private parties and weddings;
- In theatres for singers, actors, dancers and all other performers and crew;
- On the beach.

Setting Up Your Business

Setting up a new business can be a daunting task, as there are so many things to take into consideration. Some of the main questions that arise are:

- What do I call myself?
- What is my target market?
- How much do I charge?
- Where do I advertise?
- Where can I borrow money?
- How do I approach companies?
- Do I need an accountant?
- What happens about income tax?

When they first qualify, many practitioners of alternative and complementary therapies have never been in business for themselves before, and some are somewhat shy about asking for money at the end of a treatment (although this seldom lasts!). If you want to build a successful seated acupressure bodywork business you will need to approach companies in a determined, confident, and professional manner.

Before you even get that far, you will need to sit down and draw up a business plan, decide upon your goals, work out your marketing strategy, keep a book-keeping system, and how much you are going to charge. Most of the big banks will have information packs available for people who are setting up in business for the first time. If you are considering borrowing money, you will need to produce a cash flow forecast for the bank. Your Local Enterprise Agency will be able to help you with this and may run low cost or even free training courses: many accountants will also provide help and advice, especially if they think they will get your business. The Inland Revenue office in your area will also provide information about taxation and National Insurance contributions. Once you have completed your training and purchased a massage chair, the greatest cost will be your advertising. When starting to plan a business it is important to consider the following:

What will I call my business?

Business names are one of the most important factors to consider when presenting yourself to your prospective market. Your business name will feature in your advertising, on your stationery and on business cards and the first impression will be possibly the most lasting. Unless you are using your own name, it is important that whatever you decide to call your company, it conveys what you do. It is also a good idea to check other local businesses to make sure you are not using a local competitor's name or a registered business name.

How much do I charge?

When deciding on how much to charge, it is important not to have unrealistic expectations: what is a good price in one location may be far too high in another. Do some research, find out what your local competitors are charging for a similar service, and set your costs accordingly. If you charge far more you are likely to put off potential clients when you are a new business. This is equally true if you try to under-cut local practitioners by too much.

Whatever you decide to charge, make sure you are confident when approaching potential customers, and do not look as if you are unsure of your fees. If you are put on the spot about costs for an on-site contract, take the details of the job and tell the client you will work out costs and send them a quote. If you are going to be working from a clinic or shop, ensure that your charges cover costs and leave you with enough to live from.

Where do I advertise?

Decide upon your advertising budget and then work out how best to maximize it. Invest as much as you can on your stationery, business cards, letterheads, leaflets, and so on. They will look much more impressive when professionally printed. Try to include an idea of costs that might be involved. Advertising in local newspapers can be expensive but will target people in your locality. Some newspapers will give you an editorial if you book a series of adverts. This provides a good opportunity to describe what you do, possibly with pictures. These days, the best form of advertising is by having a website. A website can contain a large amount of information, pictures, and prices, etc. Websites can be accessed by anyone anywhere, and providing they are properly managed, can be one of the best ways of reaching your potential clients.

How do I approach companies?

When first making an approach to a company, it is always wise to do some sort of research. Nowadays a lot of companies will have a Health and Safety Officer and it is quite useful to contact them as well as the person in charge of Human Resources. Try to find out their names, and address any mailings directly to them. A well-written letter on good quality paper addressed to them personally explaining what it is you do will often carry more weight than a leaflet or just a telephone call. Most of the people you will have to deal with will have secretaries or personal assistants who will intercept your letters and calls so it is often beneficial to develop a good relationship with them, explaining what you can do and how you can help their company. If you make a good impression with the secretary, they will often talk to their employer and pass on your letters. Always follow up an approach by mail with a telephone call a few days later to ask if the information you sent was of any interest.

When planning and ordering your business stationery it is important to remember that your headed note-paper, business card or leaflet may be the first contact a prospective client has with you and it is wise to create a good first impression. Many printers offer business start up packs to get you going and can arrange to have any graphics designed professionally. This is a far better approach than trying to save money by printing your own stationery on an inkjet printer. If you cannot decide on a logo or business name when you first start and are going to print your stationery, at least use the best quality paper you can afford.

For more detailed marketing information, please refer to the bibliography on page 137.

The 10-Minute Routine

Back – about 3 minutes; back position / facing back

1) **Rub down** (opens channels / prepares nerves for contact)
2) **Knead shoulders** (palm of hands – firm pressure)
3) **Windscreen wipers** (using thumbs)
4) **Press muscles away from spine** (ribcage area only, muscles into spine – Kidney meridian)
5) **Kidney area / Sacral rub** (feels warm and nurturing)

Transition to front position (slide up spine, maintain contact)

Shoulders – about 1 minute; front position

1) **Knead shoulders** (first both, then work one while mother hand supports the other. Alternate rapid pressure with deep slow pressure). Key area of tension, get feedback on pressure required, this varies a lot. Use Gallbladder meridian, can release Gb21 with deep breaths and squeeze arms to open Lung meridian. Can work LI15, 11, 10.

Arms and Shoulders – about 2 minutes each; side position

1) **Shake arm** (work from top to hand – loosens shoulder joint / upper back)
2) **Squat – squeeze arm, rotate wrist** (releases and descends Qi)
3) **Standing – arm rotation** (tai chi stance; move from Hara, fingers support shoulder joint, work and support scapula, squeeze trapezius, pull shoulder back)
4) **Arm behind back** (face forwards, secure arm at elbow with your thigh, raise and rotate scapula, work SI11, 10, 8)

Arms and Hands; move to front

1) **Arm shake** (hold hand, do it gently. Mother hand supports shoulder)
2) **Arm stretch** (hand on shoulder – off bones, lean weight into shoulder and extend arm)
3) **Work hand** (rotate wrist, work back of wrist, open palm, work finger. Drains Qi powerfully from upper back / shoulder / arm. Use relevant points)

Transition; brush shoulders and then work other arm

Head – about 1 minute

1) **Knead shoulders** (Gb21, LI16)
2) **Fingertip rotation** (very gentle, work up neck into Gb20 and hold)
3) **Crab pressure** (finger pressure working occiput and up back of head)
4) **Bladder pressure** (thumbs simultaneously work the Bladder meridian up the skull to the forehead)
5) **Cradle neck** (with mother hand into occiput work into shoulder)
6) **Stroke shoulders** (nurturing, balances Qi, prepares for transition to back position)

To finish; back position – about 1 minute

1) **Rub down and stroke**
2) **Windscreen wipers / general work on the shoulders**
3) **Percussion** (use fingers / loose fists work from neck out, upper back only – not kidneys. Never on spine)
4) **Brush down and two-handed contact to finish**
5) **Sit up slowly, work shoulders** (informs client is at the end of the backrub)
6) **Eye contact** (don't ask if they liked it)

- Remember it's a backrub so do lots of rubbing down and sweeping strokes to disperse Qi;
- Only do moves with which you are comfortable. Confidence is important;
- Try to maintain two-handed contact. This provides a sense of support;
- Remember to ask if the pressure is OK. Too much pressure is better than too little. Most people like firm treatment;
- If in doubt work the shoulders.

Sample Screening and Contraindication Form

Please complete this form before your first appointment, as this will maximize the time available for the massage. Please be assured that this information will be treated with the utmost confidence. Use the reverse of the sheet if you need more space.

Name: Address: Telephone: **D.O.B.**	E-mail:	
Do you suffer from high or low blood pressure?	High / Low	If yes, *please give details.*
Do you have any of the following? Diabetes. Epilepsy. Osteoporosis.	Yes / No Yes / No Yes / No	
Have you ever suffered from tuberculosis (TB)?	Yes / No	
Do you suffer from arthritis or joint problems?	Yes / No	
Do you have any skin diseases or rashes?	Yes / No	
Have you had any recent surgery?	Yes / No	
Do you have any injuries or bruising to your upper body?	Yes / No	
Are you currently taking any medication or having any medical treatment?	Yes / No	
Do you have any communicable illness ?	Yes / No	
Are you pregnant or trying to conceive? *This form of massage is not suitable for pregnant women. If your circumstances change you must inform me.*	Yes / No	
Have you ever been advised not to have massage?	Yes / No	
Notes:		
Please sign and date this form.		

Treatment Record

	Date	Feedback from previous treatments and observations or notes from this session.
Name:		
1		
2		
3		
4		
5		
6		
7		
8		
9		
10		

Summary of the 20-Minute Seated Acupressure Bodywork Sequence

Opening Contact

Make two-handed contact with your client's upper back and shoulder.

Double Palm Press

Palm down the middle of the erector spinae muscles in five equally spaced positions.

Kneading

Using your palms, thumbs and fingers, knead the shoulders.

Stretching Away From the Spine

Using both hands, with the heel of the
hand in the hollow between the spine and
the muscles, press the muscles away from
the spine

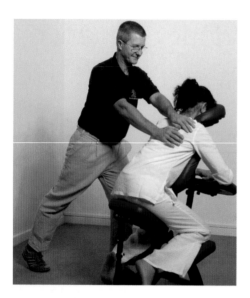

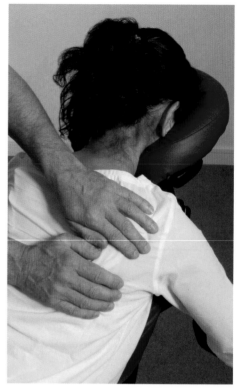

Archer's Arm

Drop your weight down through your arm
to apply pressure through the heel of your
hand, your fingers should be facing away
from the spine.

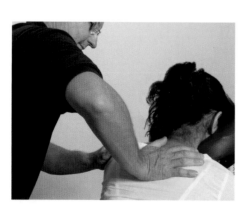

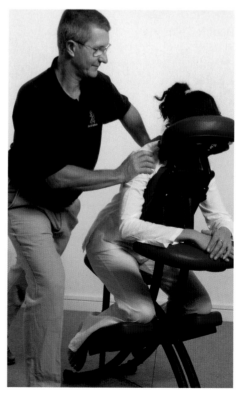

Forearm Press

Stand slightly in front of your client and sink into the trapezius muscle with the soft underside of your forearm.

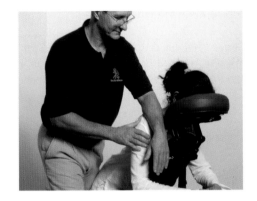

Elbow Press to Nine Points

It is important to ensure your client is comfortable with the pressure when using this technique. Keep your wrists loose and your elbow at a right angle to the back. Lean your body weight into your front leg to apply the pressure.

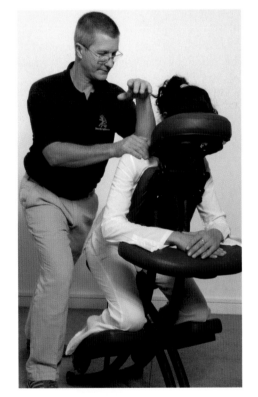

Forearm Rolling

Roll your forearm as you work down the medial border of the scapula.

Elbow Press

Step forward and drop your weight down through your elbow into three evenly spaced points between the neck and the acromioclavicular joint.

Arm Shake

Shake or roll the arm between the palms of your hands, working from shoulder to wrist.

Thumb Squeeze

Squeeze the muscle between your thumb and forefingers, rolling it slightly towards you. Work five points down the upper arm.

Thumb Press

Bring both hands up to the level of the axilla and grip the biceps brachii and triceps brachii muscles by placing the thumbs together on the side of the arm. Squeeze five points in this way, working down the upper arm.

Wrist Flex and Squeeze

Supporting above their wrist with both hands, flick the wrist back and forth. Using your left hand to support their wrist, take hold of their fingers and rotate gently in both directions. Then flex and extend the wrist to gently stretch the tendons. Squeeze the sides of the wrist between your thumb and index finger.

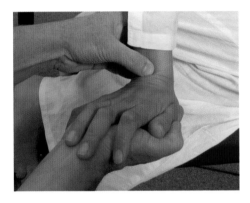

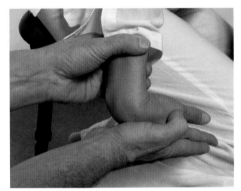

Shoulder Rotations

Scoop up their arm supporting under their elbow and support their shoulder with your hand. Place your other hand over the scapula and circle their shoulder, rotating their arm in a backwards direction. Repeat several times.

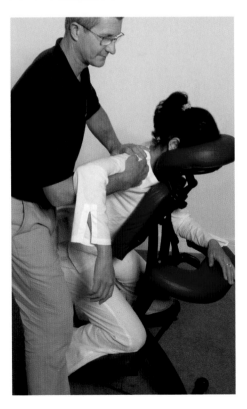

Chicken Wing – Thumbs Under Scapula

Lower their arm and bring it behind their back into the chicken wing position. Draw the scapula back onto your thumb or fingers.

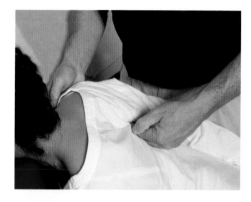

Hand Spread, Thumb Strokes and Jiggles

Spread open the back of the hand using the heels of your hand. With the pads of your thumbs stroke down between the outer metacarpals of the hand. Then 'jiggle' your thumbs between the outer metacarpals. Repeat this with the inner metacarpals.

Palm Spread and Stretch

Spread open the palm of your client's hand using the heels of your hands, and linking your little fingers between their thumb and index finger, and ring and little fingers. Stretch out their palm and work the thenar and hypothenar eminences with your thumbs.

Coin Rubs

Rub briskly down from the base of the thumb to the tip, as if polishing a coin between your fingers and thumb, pulling towards you slightly.

Nail Point Squeeze

Squeeze the nail points between your thumb and forefinger for a second.

Fingertip Snap

Bring your index finger onto the nail and squeeze their finger between the second and third fingers. Pull off briskly with a snap.

Arm Stretch

Bring their arm around to the front of their body. Step forward far enough to allow you to stretch their arm forward whilst supporting under their elbow with your left hand and at their wrist with your right.

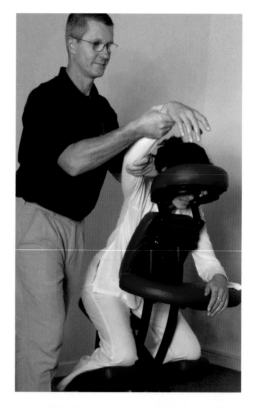

Single Palm Press

Place the heel of your hand over the erector spinae muscle on one side of the spine, with your fingers cupping lightly over the spinal column. Place your other hand lightly on the shoulder. Press down five equally spaced points, beginning at about the level of T8/T9 and finishing just above the iliac crest.

Thumb Press to Nine Points

Stand directly behind your client. Supporting your right thumb in between your left thumb and index finger, press down onto nine evenly spaced points along the erector spinae muscle to the left of the spine.

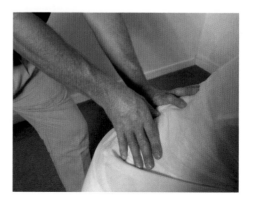

Palm Rotations and Sacral Rub

Position yourself behind your client and place your palm over the sacrum. Brace your elbow on the inside of your own thigh. Rotate your palm slowly in an upward and outwards circle. Repeat three times. The contact should be fairly firm and you should imagine you are moving their flesh over the bone rather than just brushing your hand over the surface of their sacrum.

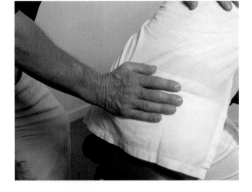

Brush Down

Brush down the top of the back to the bottom. Then slide both hands up to the shoulders.

Dragon's Mouth

With your hand lightly gripping the neck, gently squeeze five equally spaced points along the neck just lateral to the cervical vertebrae. Allow your hands to gently roll towards you while working down this line.

Shoulder Kneading With Occipital Support

Facing the top of the client's head, cradle the occiput with one hand and knead their shoulder with the other. Knead with the heel of your hand, between thumb and four fingers and pressing away.

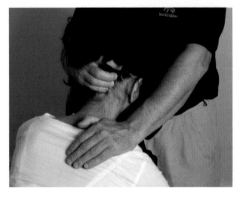

Spider Press-ups

Using your fingertips, work up into their scalp as if washing their hair. Imagine your fingers are spiders doing press-ups.

Crab Grabs

Use the pads of your fingers to grip the scalp and pull away quickly. Repeat this several times.

Karate Chop Hacking

Using the sides of your hands, 'karate chop' style, hack across the back from the centre line to the edge of the trapezius muscle and back. Then hack in a line down the erector spinae muscle to the lower end of the ribcage and back again. Repeat twice on each side of the spine. This will form a T shaped pattern.

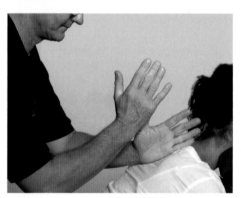

Prayer Hands Hacking

Pressing the palms of you hands together (prayer hands), hack across the back in a similar movement to the previous technique. This gives slightly more weight to the technique.

Loose Fist Hacking, Curled Fist or Cupped Hands Percussion

Form loose fists or cupped hands and repeat the above movement twice. When using the cupped hands, they should be lightly clasped palm to palm, and on connecting with the back should make a squishing noise. The emphasis should be on lifting off the body rather than on the downward stroke.

Double Forearm Press

Move back behind them and place your forearms on their shoulders and gently press down. Be very careful not to press too hard and exaggerate their natural lumbar curve and compress the vertebrae.

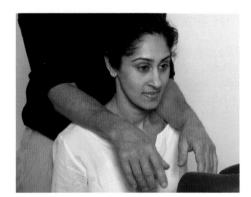

Neck Stretch

Leaving your left arm in place, place your right arm over their head so your fingers are by their left ear. Gently draw their head over to the right as far as it will naturally go (explain to them what you are going to do). Ask them to take a deep breath in. As they breathe out, gently stretch down on their left shoulder.

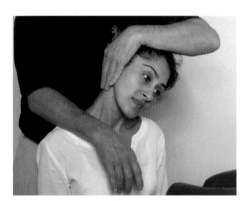

Penguin Stretch

Reach under their elbows from the back and take hold of their forearms. Ask them to inhale. As they exhale, stretch backwards and upwards.

Angel Stretch

Bring their arms up in a circular movement until they can clasp their hands behind their head. Reach up under their arms. Ask them to inhale, and as they exhale, stretch their arms backwards.

Shoulder Drop

Clasp both their shoulders and as they inhale, and raise both their shoulders simultaneously. Ask them to exhale and at some point during the exhalation, drop their shoulders.

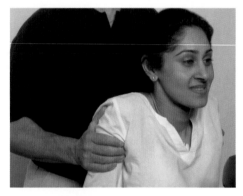

Closing Brush Strokes

Brush across the shoulders a couple of times and then again down the back.

Grounding Your Client

Finish off by either connecting with their low back and across C7/T1, or by kneeling behind them and contacting Kidney 3 and Bladder 60 bilaterally. (These points are located on either side of the ankles, between the malleoli and the Achilles tendon).

Summary of the 20-Minute Seated Acupressure Bodywork Sequence

Back			Low Back		
Opening contact			Double palm press – scapulae	5 positions	x2
Double palm press	5 positions	x2	to sacrum		
Shoulder kneading			Single palm press – left side	5 positions	x2
Pressing away from spine			Double thumb press down		
(both sides)	3 positions	x2	Bladder channel	9 positions	x2
Archer's arm (palm press)	3 positions	x2			
Forearm press	9 positions	x2	*Repeat on the right*		
Elbow into Bladder channel	4 positions	x2			
Scapula border	3 positions	x2	Thumb press on sacrum	4 positions	x2
Elbow press on shoulder					
			Sacrum and Buttocks		
Upper Arm			Palm rotations		
Roll and shake the arm			Left hand on sacrum	3 rotations	x1
Biceps brachii squeeze	5 positions	x2	Left hand on gluteus muscle	3 rotations	x1
Triceps brachii squeeze	5 positions	x2	Right hand on gluteus muscle	3 rotations	x1
Thumb press	5 positions	x2	Right hand on sacrum	3 rotations	x1
Lower Arm			Brush down from shoulders		x3 / 4
Thumb press: radius	5 positions	x2	to sacrum		
ulna	5 positions	x2			
Between radius and ulna	5 positions	x2	**Neck and Head**		
Squeeze and rotate wrist			Left side	5 points	
			Fingers under occiput	5 points	x2
Shoulder Rotations			Neck points, 3 lines	3 points	x2
Scoop up arm			Crest of trapezius		x2
Rotate shoulder joint		x3	Brush across shoulders		
Rotate shoulder girdle		x3			
Swing arm behind back			*Repeat on right side*		
Fingers / thumbs under scapula					
Place arm on armrest			Cradle occiput / knead left shoulder		
Spread back of hand			Cradle occiput / knead right shoulder		
Stroke and jiggle between					
the outer / inner metacarpals		x2	Hook fingers under occiput		
Press LI4		x2			
			Fingertips into scalp		
Turn palm face up			Spider press-ups		
Thumb press from elbow			Bladder channel in head		
to wrist crease					
Ulnar line (Heart channel)		x2	Brush shoulders		
Medial line (HP channel)	5 positions	x2			
Radial line (Lung channel)	5 positions	x2	Hacking on back		x2
Link fingers and spread palm	5 positions				
Stroke and jiggle between					
the outer / inner metacarpals		x2	Brush down		x2
Press Lu10		x2			
			Sit client upright		
Coin rub fingers from thumb to			Shoulder press		
little finger, squeeze nail point,			Neck stretch right and left		
and finish with finger snap			Chicken wing stretch		x1
			Angel stretch		x1
Lance stretch			Knead shoulders		x1
Repeat on right side from			Shoulder drop		
Archer's arm position		x1	Brush down		x2
			Finish on Ki3 or low back / C7		x3

A Guide to Cun Measurements

Cun are units of measurement used to locate
acupressure points on the body. Each figure/number
relates to a cun measurement.

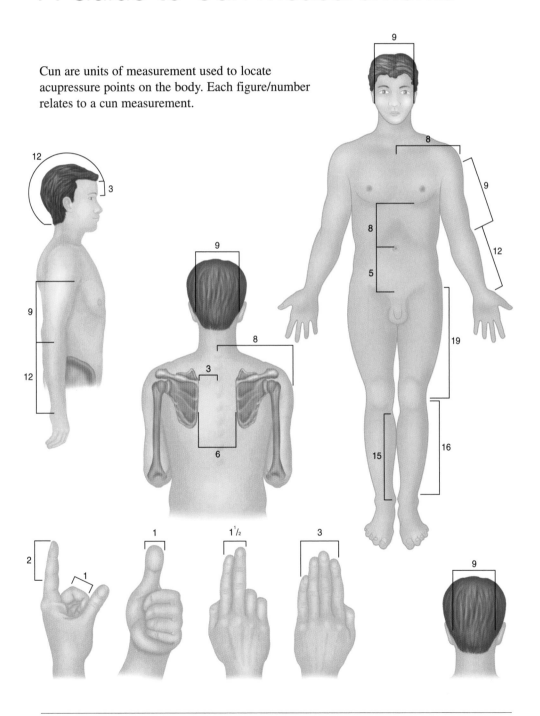

Bibliography

Abercromby, P., Thomson, D.: 2005. *Seated Acupressure Therapy: from Ancient Art to Modern Practice.* Corpus Publishing, Gloucester

Fontana, D.: 1989. *Managing Stress.* The British Psychology Society / Routledge, London

Harold, S.: 2005. *Marketing Tips for Complementary Therapists.* How to Books, Oxford

Jarmey, C.: 2004. *The Atlas of Musculo-skeletal Anatomy.* Lotus Publishing / North Atlantic Books, Chichester / Berkeley

Jarmey, C., Mojay, G.: 1991. *Shiatsu: the Complete Guide.* Harper Collins, London

Jarmey, C., and Tindall, J.: 2005. *Acupressure for Common Ailments.* Gaia Books, London

Kaptchuk, T. J.: 2000. *The Web That Has No Weaver.* Contemporary Books, Inc., New York

Kirsa, A.: 1987. *The Book of Stress Survival: Identifying and Reducing the Stress in Your Life.* Prentice Hall, London

Looker, T., Gregson, O.: 2003. *Managing Stress.* Hodder & Stoughton, London

Maciocia, G.: 1997. *The Foundations of Chinese Medicine: A Comprehensive Text for Acupuncturists and Herbalists.* Churchill Livingstone, Edinburgh

Niel-Asher, S.: 2005. *The Concise Book of Trigger Points.* Lotus Publishing / North Atlantic Books, Chichester / Berkeley

Patel, C.: 1996. *The Complete Guide to Stress Management.* Ebury Press, London

Pyves, G., Woodhouse, D.: 2003. *No Hands Chair Massage.* Shi'Zen Publications, Hebden Bridge

Useful Addresses

Academy of Massage Therapy
401 South van Brunt St., Suite 204
Englewood, NJ 07631, USA
Tel.: 1-888-ATT-7898
www.academyofmassage.com

Academy of Seated Acupressure Therapy
Avon Road, Charfield
Wotton-under-Edge, GL12 8TT, UK
Tel.: 01454 269269
www.aosm.co.uk

Backrubbers
Unit 11. The Enterprise Centre
Station Parade
Eastbourne, BN21 1BD, UK
Tel.: 01323 430025
info@backrubbers.co.uk

College of Integrated Chinese Medicine
19. Castle Street
Reading, RG1 7SB, UK
Tel.: 0118 950 8880
www.cicm.org.uk

Embody
2nd floor, Chiswick Gate
598–608 Chiswick High Road
London, W4 5RT, UK
Tel.: 0870 201 4260
www.embodyforyou.com

The European Shiatsu School
Branches throughout the UK,
Eire, Greece and Spain
Central Administration: Highbank,
Lockeridge, Marlborough, SN8 4EQ, UK
Tel.: 0845 166 5144
www.shiatsu.net

Injury Prevention Ltd.,
22. High Street, Normanton
WF6 2AB, UK
Tel.: 01924 223 225
www.injuryprevention.org.uk
also suppliers of Earthlite chairs and couches

Seated Acupressure Training School
82. The Spinney
Beaconsfield, HP9 1SA, UK
Tel.: 01494 678221
www.acupressure-training.co.uk

Sister Rosalind Schools and Clinics of Massage
149 E. Thompson Ave., Suite 160
West St. Paul, MN 55118, USA
Tel.: (651) 554-3010
www.sisterrosalind.org

TouchPro Institute
584 Castro Street #555
San Francisco, CA 94114, USA
Tel.: 880-999-5026 (USA / Canada)
www.touchpro.com

TouchPro UK
176. Melrose Avenue, London
NW2 4JY, UK
Tel.: 0208 450 3366
www.touchpro.org

Walk-in BackRub
11. Charlotte Place, London
W1T 1SJ, UK
Tel.: 0207 436 9875
www.walkinbackrub.co.uk

Manufacturers and Suppliers of Chairs

Darley Couches
5. Restormel Estate
Lostwithiel, PL22 0HG, UK
Tel.: 01208 873200
www.darleycouches.co.uk

**Golden Ratio Spa & Bodywork
Equipment & Supplies**
P O Box 440,
Emigrant, MT 59027, USA
www.goldenratio.com

Marshcouch
14. Robinsfield, Hemel Hempstead
HP1 1RW, UK
Tel.: 01442 263199
www.marshcouch.com

The Massage Table Store
Unit P2, Bow Wharf, Grove Road
London E3 5SN, UK
Tel.: 0208 983 9800
www.mts4u.com
Suppliers of a variety of massage chairs and
couches including the Oakworks Portal Pro

Oakworks, Inc.
923 E. Wellspring Rd.
New Freedom, PA 17349 or
P O Box 238,
Shrewsbury, PA 17361–0238, USA
Tel.: 717.235.6807
Toll free 800.916.4613
www.oakworks.net

Index

Acupressure points 9, 18
Adrenaline 29
Adrenocorticotrophic hormone (ACTH) 29
Advertise 115
Aftercare advice 97
Alcohol 38
Angel stretch 91, 132
Angry cat 105
Anma 7
Archer's arm 52, 66, 122
Arm shake 56, 70, 124
Arm stretch 59, 64, 73, 78, 128
Arthritis 38
Ashi points 18

Back exercises 103
Bladder meridian 16, 20, 21
Breathing 97, 98
Broken bones 38
Bruising 39
Brush down 82, 87, 89, 129
Brush strokes 92, 132
Business, setting up your 114

Cancer 39
Cannon, Walter 29
Charge 115
Chicken wing 59, 73, 126
Child's pose 105
Clients 35
Coin rubs 63, 77, 127
Common mistakes 95
Communication skills 41
Conception vessel 16
Contraindications 35, 37, 119
Control cycle 13, 14
Corticosteroids 29
Cosmological cycle 15

Crab grabs 86, 130
Creation cycle 13, 14
Cross stitch percussion 89
Cun 135
Cupped hands percussion *see* curled
    hand percussion
Curled fist percussion 89, 131

Diabetes 39
Diet 34
Do-in self-massage exercises 101
Double forearm press 90, 131
Double palm press 50, 80, 87, 121
Dragon's mouth 84, 129
Dress 41

Earth 12, 13
Edo period 7
Effleurage 108
Elbow press 54, 68, 124
Elbow press to nine points 53, 67, 123
Epilepsy 39
Equipment 44

Feedback 36
Fight-or-flight response 29, 30
Fingertip snap 63, 77, 127
Fire 12, 13
Five elements 11
Five phase theory *see* five element theory
Forearm press 52, 66, 123
Forearm rolling 54, 68, 123
Friction 112
Frictions 112

Gallbladder meridian 16, 23
Governing vessel 16
Grounding your client 92, 132

Hacking 88

Hand spread 60, 74, 126

Hara 101

Heart disease 39

Heart meridian 16, 25

Heart protector meridian 16, 26

High blood pressure 39

Holmes-Rahe social adjustment scale 30

Huang-ti 7

Hygiene 42

Hypothalamus-pituitary-adrenal
    (HPA) axis 29

Karate chop hacking 130

Kata 8, 18

Ke cycle *see* control cycle

Kidney meridian 16

Kneading 51, 121

Knee to chest tuck 104

Large intestine meridian 16, 22

Legs, working the 93

Lifestyle 33

Liver meridian 16

Low blood pressure 39

Low blood sugar 39

Lung meridian 16, 27

Maintenance advice 100

Meridians 9, 15

Metal 12, 13

Multifidis strengthening exercise 105

Musculo-skeletal problems 38

Nail point squeeze 63, 77, 127

Neck stretch 90, 131

Negative stress response 29

Noradrenaline 29

Observations 35

Occipital release 86

Opening contact 50, 121

Osteoporosis 39

Palmer, David 7

Palm rotations and sacral rub 82, 129

Palm spread and stretch 62, 76, 126

Pelvic tilt 104

Penguin stretch 91, 131

Percussion techniques 88

Personal care 42

Petrissage 108

Pituitary gland 29

Point locations,
    inner aspect of the left arm and hand 61
    inner aspect of the right arm and hand 75
    left shoulder and upper back 49
    lower back and sacrum 79
    neck and head 83
    outer aspect of the left arm and hand 55
    outer aspect of the right arm and hand 69
    right shoulder and upper back 65

Posture 36, 47

Prayer hands 88, 130

Pregnancy 40

Progressive muscular relaxation (PMR) 99

Promotional material 45

Qi 9

Record keeping 36, 42

Recreational drugs 38

Relaxation 97

Routine,
    inner aspect of the left arm and hand 62
    inner aspect of the right arm and hand 76
    left shoulder and upper back 50
    lower back and sacrum 80
    neck and head 84
    outer aspect of the left arm and hand 56
    outer aspect of the right arm and hand 70
    right shoulder and upper back 66

Sacral points 81

Screening 35, 119

Seiza 98

Shaking 111

Sheng cycle *see* creation cycle

Shiatsu 8

Shoulder drop 92, 132

Shoulder kneading 64, 78, 82, 85, 129

Shoulder rotations 58, 72, 125

Single knee to chest stretch 104

Single palm press 81, 128

Skin diseases 40

Small intestine meridian 16, 19

Spider press-ups 86, 130
Spinal twists 105
Spleen meridian 16
Stomach 16
Stress 29, 97
Stressors 29
Stretching 103
Stretching away from the spine 51, 122

T'ai-ji symbol 10
Tapotement 110
Technique 37
Tendonitis 33
Tenosynovitis 33
Thrombosis 40
Thumb press 57, 62, 71, 76, 81, 84, 85,
   124, 128
Thumbs along bladder channel 87
Thumb squeeze 56, 70, 124
Thumb strokes 63, 77
Triple heater meridian 16, 24
Tsubos *see* acupressure points
Tuberculosis 40

Upper limb disorders 33

Vibrations 111

Warming lower back 80
Water 12
Wood 12
Working environment 41
Work-related stress 30, 32
Wrist flex and squeeze 58, 72, 125

Yang 10, 15
Ying 10, 15

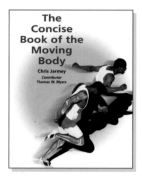

The Concise Book of the Moving Body

Chris Jarmey with **Thomas W. Myers**; 1 905367 01 5 (UK); 1 55643 623 8 (US); **£16.99/$29.95**; 192 pages; 275 mm x 212 mm; 250 colour illustrations; paperback

The Concise Book of the Moving Body is a compact reference guide, clearly detailing anatomical orientation, tissues, in-depth information on joints, and the physiology of bones and muscles. Composite drawings of the body illustrate the major skeletal muscles (posterior and anterior, superficial and deep), including the origin, insertion, innervation, and action for each muscle.

A final chapter by Thomas W. Myers outlines several metaphors helpful to a holistic approach to structural and movement therapies, and describes a map of the larger functioning continuities within the musculo-skeletal system.

Chris Jarmey, M.C.S.P., D.S., M.R.S.S., qualified as a Chartered Physiotherapist in 1979. He is the author of several best-selling books, including *The Concise Book of Muscles*, and *The Atlas of Musculo-skeletal Anatomy* also published by Lotus Publishing and North Atlantic Books. Jarmey teaches body mechanics, bodywork therapy, and anatomy extensively throughout Europe.

Thomas W. Myers, L.M.T., N.C.T.M.B., A.R.P., is a licensed massage therapist and certified advanced Rolf practitioner. Myers gives frequent workshops throughout the USA and in Europe. He is the author of *Anatomy Trains* (Churchill Livingstone) and has published several series of articles in both *Massage* magazine and the *Journal of Bodywork and Movement Therapies*.

"A very comprehensive book, which provides an in-depth study of the muscular system as well as the skeletal system. Well researched, well planned, and beautifully illustrated...a must-have for students and practitioners alike."
Mario-Paul Cassar, D.O., N.D., practitioner and teacher in osteopathy, bodywork, clinical massage, and sports therapy; author of the *Handbook of Clinical Massage* (Churchill Livingstone).

The Theory and Practice of Taiji Qigong

Chris Jarmey; 0 9543188 2 X (UK); 1 55643 554 1 (US); **£10.99/$18.95**; 192 pages; 246 mm x 189 mm; 160 line drawings; paperback

Taiji Qigong is an easy-to-learn system of energy-enhancing exercises which co-ordinates movement with breathing and inner concentration. Taiji Qigong is widely practiced throughout the Far East and increasingly throughout the Western world. Research indicates that Qigong relaxes the muscles and nervous system (so improving the function of other body systems) and benefits posture, balance and flexibility of joints.

This book acts as an in-depth instruction manual for the practice of the 18 Stances of Taiji Qigong. The book is written with all levels and depths of practice in mind, and is constructed so that you can take from it the necessary information and techniques to suite your own individual goals. The book covers the theory of Qi and Qigong; the general principles of Qigong practice; and the 18 movements of Taiji Qigong in detail.

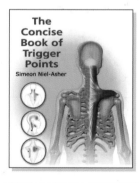

The Concise Book of Trigger Points

Simeon Neil-Asher; 0 9543188 5 4 (UK); 1 55643 536 3 (US); **£16.99/$29.95**; 208 pages; 275 mm x 212 mm; 240 colour illustrations; paperback

The Concise Book of Trigger Points has been written for the student and early practitioner of massage / bodywork, physical therapy, physiotherapy, osteopathy, sports therapy, and any other health-related field. It is a compact reference guide and explains how to treat chronic pain through trigger points. The first four chapters provide a sound background to the physiology of trigger points, and the general methods of treatment. The following six chapters are organized by muscle groups: each two-page spread features detailed colour illustrations of each major skeletal muscle, and text identifying each muscle's origin, insertion, action, and function. In addition, the author discusses the physiological implications of the trigger points in each muscle, and techniques for treatment.

Simeon Niel-Asher B. Phil., B.Sc., (Ost.), is involved in treating, research, writing, and teaching throughout Europe, the Middle East, and the USA.

"This book represents an excellent entry level text which will be a powerful learning aid to any student or newly qualified practitioner. All schools providing courses that include any aspect of trigger points should place this book on their recommended book list."
John Sharkey, B.Sc., Neuromuscular Therapist, Director, National Training Centre, Ireland.

**Orders: For the UK, Europe : any branch of Waterstones / amazon.co.uk.
For the USA, Canada, Australia, New Zealand : northatlanticbooks.com / amazon.com.**